Dissonant Pieties

Dissonant Pieties

John Calvin and the Prayer Psalms of the Psalter

Paul A. Riemann

Foreword by Walter Brueggemann

CASCADE *Books* • Eugene, Oregon

DISSONANT PIETIES
John Calvin and the Prayer Psalms of the Psalter

Cascade Books
An Imprint of Wipf and Stock Publishers
199 W. 8th Ave., Suite 3
Eugene, OR 97401

www.wipfandstock.com

ISBN 13: 978-1-62032-556-8

Cataloguing-in-Publication data:

Riemann, Paul Alfonso, 1933–.

Dissonant pieties : John Calvin and the prayer Psalms of the Psalter / Paul A. Riemann ; foreword by Walter Brueggemann.

xx + **82** pp. ; 23 cm. Includes bibliographical references and indexes.

ISBN 13: 978-1-62032-556-8

1. Bible. Psalms—Criticism, interpretation, etc.—History—16th century. 2. Calvin, Jean. 3. Prayer—Biblical teaching. I. Brueggemann, Walter. II. Title.

BS1445 M4 R5 2014

Manufactured in the U.S.A.

Reprinted, with permission, from *Inspired Speech: Prophecy in the Ancient Near East. Essays in Honour of Herbert B. Huffmon*, edited by John Kaltner and Louis Stulman, London: T. & T. Clark, 2004.

For my wife, Joy Drexel Reber Riemann,
in gratitude for her love and support
for more than fifty-two years.

Although David intended to submit completely to God's will, and prayed with no less patience than zeal to obtain his request, yet there come forth—sometimes, rather, boil up—turbulent emotions, quite out of harmony with the first rule that we laid down.

—CALVIN, *INSTITUTES*, 3.20.16

Contents

Foreword

LARRY BROWN, THE MUCH traveled and much winning basketball coach, is fond of saying over and over that basketball must be played "in the right way." By that Coach Brown means attention to the fundamentals . . . pass and dribble, pick and roll, shoot and rebound . . . no frills, no tricks, no exhibitionism. But clearly he also means by "the right way" to do it the way Brown says to do it, as he is not filled with self- doubt. John Calvin, in that regard, is a lot like Larry Brown. Calvin insists we should pray "in the right way." By that Calvin means to take the fundamentals. He likely would agree with Karl Barth's sense that "prayer or praying is simply asking.[1] To that formulation of Barth, Calvin would only add that "asking" must be done reverently, submissively, and confidently. But Calvin also means, like Brown, to do it the way Calvin says to do it, as he is also is not filled with self-doubt.

Calvin exposits "the right way" to pray in Book III of his *Institutes of Christian Religion*, the "book" that is titled: "The Way in which We Receive the Grace of Christ: What Benefits Come to Us from It, and What Effects Follow."[2] I discovered that I had his four "rules" for prayer underlined from my earlier reading in my copy of the *Institutes*, but was no longer mindful of the rules nor that I had read them until I was reminded of it by Paul Riemann. Riemann's essay that follows here offers a fair and accessible presentation of

---

1. Barth, *Church Dogmatics* III/3, 268. He writes of the asking: "And both with heart and mouth the asking of the community which is elected together with Him will be a true and genuine asking . . . Thus the asking community stands together with its Lord before God on behalf of all creation" (277, 279).

2. Calvin, *Institutes of the Christian Religion* [1559 edition].

Calvin's exposition, and indicates his own empathetic reading of Calvin's way of thinking about prayer.

But of course Riemann's study does much more than review Calvin. He joins issue with Calvin through his term "dissonant" to show: a) the way in which Calvin could not accept what he found in the "piety" of the Psalter; and b) the ways he found either to counteract that piety or explain it away. In my own work on a Psalms commentary I recently read through Calvin's commentary as I wrote my own. I had noticed, with reference to specific Psalms, the same tendency on the part of Calvin that Riemann identifies. But I had not named it for myself nor recognized the systemic force of his interpretive stance when taken as a whole. When I read Riemann's essay, it struck me as a most remarkable, important, and welcome study, surely the most remarkable essay in the fine collection honoring Herbert Huffmon.[3] I am delighted that it is now republished in a much more accessible form. I anticipate that it will become an important critical tool, both for reflection upon the Psalms and for engagement with Calvin's theological propensity.

Calvin lived, as the Reformation required, in a moment when the claims of the biblical text were no longer easily silenced by the weight of the dogmatic traditions of the church. With Luther's *sola scriptura*, there could be an attempt, a game-changing attempt, to see that the Bible itself had a voice other than the one permitted by settled church tradition. The *sola scriptura* of theological interpretation was, of course, accompanied by the rise of historical criticism of which Calvin's own work was an important harbinger. He moved well beyond the well established work of allegory and typology which Luther more readily continued to practice toward a closer "historical sense" of the text. Indeed there is some irony in Calvin's attempt to take the Old Testament on its own terms. Pak has explored the way in which Calvin, in his treatment of "messianic Psalms," was accused of being a "Judaizer" because he credited Jewish understandings of such Psalms.[4] Thus he took some first steps toward a modern, critical reading of the Psalms.

3. Kaltner and Stulman, eds., *Inspired Speech: Prophecy in the Ancient Near East: Essays in Honour of Herbert B. Huffmon.*

4. Pak, *The Judaizing Calvin.*

For all of that, however, Calvin was committed to his systematic theology that is offered in his *Institutes* and that is inevitably reflected as well in his commentary on the Psalms. Concerning the vexed question of the interrelation of human freedom, divine freedom, and human responsibility, he focused, for good pastoral reason in his context of Pelagian ecclesiology, on a high claim for divine sovereignty. As a result, he could not countenance the much more dialogical practice of the Psalms and the vigorous covenantal ways of faith that pervade the Old Testament and that show up in on-going rabbinic playfulness. He could not see the legitimacy of practices of faith that challenged more settled convictions about God, God's sovereignty, and God's providential care. And when such voices are sounded in the Psalms, he found them not to be expressions serious faith but a flawed expression of feeble and frail people who could not measure up to the expectations of responsible faith.

The "dissonant" dimension that Riemann identifies in Calvin's interpretation of the Psalms is a paradigmatic case of the seemingly insoluble tension between exegesis and theological systematic interpretation, a tension that is still powerful among us, as is evident, for example, in the new commentary series of *The Church's Bible* (Eerdmans). That series is offered by systematic theologians who view biblical interpretation as too important to be left to the exegetes. The effect in some sense is a return to pre-critical reading. It continues, in such work, to be the case in such studies, as with Calvin, that the text is sometimes "required," at the hands of theologians, to say certain things in the service of faith, even when the text itself incontestably says otherwise. And in the practice of the church, in its hymns and prayers moreover, the systematic interpretation of the text most often prevails. Daniel Driver has recently shown that Brevard Childs, perhaps a model interpreter in our time in the tradition of Calvin, walked a fine line and could not finally arrive at a good solution, sometimes being an exegete who took the text as text even against theological "requirement," but who sometimes accepted instead systematic theological conclusions.[5]

---

5. Driver, *Brevard Childs, Biblical Theologian.*

Childs is simply a contemporary case in point of the continuing problematic of interpretation, a problematic that is, to be sure, part of the legacy of Calvin, but that is in fact evident in every serious theological tradition. Thus there is a strange alienation between *the oddity of biblical testimony* and *the requirements of established ecclesial tradition* that seems always tempted to reductionism and closure. Riemann shows that Calvin is exactly a paradigmatic figure in that strange alienation that he chose to settle in his own preferred way. But Riemann demonstrates that Calvin's preferred way is exceedingly difficult in the face of textual testimony. It will be important, after Riemann's remarkable study, to continue to assess the enduring losses and liabilities that have come in the wake of Calvin's work.

Riemann's study invites us to consider the alternative piety of the Psalms that dissents from that of Calvin and from much of the conventional ecclesial tradition. From such a perspective, the verses in the Psalms to which Calvin objects are not to be dismissed as failed faith. These include statements of abrasive demand, or irreverent accusation against God, and of wished-for vengeance against one's enemies, in short, all of the verses that give free, unembarrassed expression to "regressive" emotive sensibility. They are, as Riemann suggests in a way that makes sense to me, rather than failed faith, exercises in honesty that assume some privilege and entitlement in the presence of God: to tell the truth about themselves, and to tell the truth about God as it is given in their own lives, without deference to settled conviction. Such statements that recur in the Psalms are very often not unlike the confrontation between *Job's experience* and *Job's settled theological tradition* voiced by his friends. In the book of Job, that tension and contest is overcome only by the whirlwind speeches of God that exhibit God emancipated from the close moral calculus of the friends. Indeed Job, in his consternation, has spoken "what is right" (Job 42:7–8). In Riemann's presentation, Calvin is cast as one of the "friends" who do not want the realities of lived experience of the faithful to be voiced, but want instead that such experience should be reverently "submitted" to the truth of God already given.

It is clear that in practice Calvin and his systematic propensity have largely won the day, for the Psalms of such challenging candor have mostly disappeared from church practice, or must be bowdlerized in order to be acceptable. Like the good exegete that he is, Riemann suggests, against the weight of much shared wisdom, that the very verses to which Calvin objects are in fact the offer and performance of an alternative form of serious faith that cannot and will not be coaxed or pressured into the preferred categories of Calvin. Fortunately we are able to see that such aggressive candor in the presence of God can be taken with theological seriousness as in the case of the so-called Pastoral Care Movement. That enterprise has been initiated and has flourished in the last two generations as a kind of subversion of dominant theological settlements. Its practitioners have recognized in their own lives, in the lives of their "clients," and in the lives of their students that the lived reality of people's lives does not readily conform to the settled tradition of Calvin's way—and the way of the church. Troubled human experience is not reducible to guilt that too readily goes along with submissive reverence. This subversion subverts the dominant version of human reality and offers a sub-version that focuses on unresolved pain. The Pastoral Care Movement has come to understand and to recover an awareness that guilt is in fact a secondary emotion that is frequently laid on top of the primary experience of pain. Pain is much more elemental than is guilt, and pain must be honored if it is to be eased and finally healed. But pain freely expressed comes to voice, as in the Psalms, as abrasive, impatient, demanding, and often filled with rage. Such pain refuses to be silenced in reverence or as guilt. We now have to come to see not only that such pain is the truth of our lives, but that it makes sense theologically. The breath-taking exposition of God's pathos by Abraham Heschel has permitted us to ponder the interface between human pain that may be expressed in violent ways and God's own pain that in the prophets was voiced with profound abrasiveness.[6] But much settled theological tradition refuses such a rearticulation of God in light of that reality, a rearticulation that refuses settled sovereignty in a way

6. Heschel, *The Prophets*. In the wake of Heschel came Moltmann, *The Crucified God*, and Kitamori, *The Theology of the Pain of God*.

that draws God into the dialogical enterprise in which both parties are at risk and both parties are deeply impinged upon by such a voicing.[7]

What we have learned in recent pastoral theology, as Riemann shows, is already fully acknowledged and practiced in the piety of the Psalms. The Psalter, when its preponderance of laments and complaints is taken seriously, offers a first response to trouble that shuns submissiveness and reverence that inevitably run the risk of denial. Whatever Israel did in prayer, it ran no risks of denial! Taking a cue from the fact that almost all complaints end in praise, Erhard Gerstenberger has proposed that such Psalms are scripts for "rituals of rehabilitation" that were performed in village life, away from the temple with its propensity to uninterrupted doxology.[8] That is, the complaints serve rehabilitation. Something is accomplished through the performance of this script that can only be done with the honest offer of regressive truth-telling. The matter is reiterated over and over in the very Psalms with which Calvin had the most misgivings. Not without reason, moreover, it has been recognized that what has been practiced in Twelve Step Programs for rehabilitation and even Kubler-Ross's more questionable "Stages of Grief" is clearly anticipated in the practice of the Psalter. If we can get behind the accent on "submissiveness and reverence," we may be astonished by an awareness that the Psalter already fully understood the dynamics of transformation through candor when that candor is honored and taken seriously. In my own reading, I believe that the most important discussion of the matter, difficult and inaccessible as it is, is the study of Fredrick Lindstrom who has made the case that the lament psalms contain almost no statement of guilt.[9] That is, troubled Israel did not accept blame for its trouble (Even the seven so-called "Penitential Psalms," except for 51, do not go very far in the direction of submissive reverence.):

"It is highly doubtful if we can speak of a motif of sin in the individual complaint psalms, which it is supposed to function in

---

7. See Brueggemann, *An Unsettling God*, 1–17, on "YHWH as Dialogical Character."

8. Gerstenberger, *Der Bittende Mensch*.

9. Lindstrom, *Suffering and Sin*.

the supposed way. The confession of sin is not an element in the classical individual complaint psalm, and the motif of sin, in the few cases in which it occurs, hardly functions as an indication of the reason for the affliction."[10]

Instead of accepting fault before God, Israel can claim either that its trouble is because of assault by an enemy (unnamed but fully in purview) or that Israel (or the speaker) has been abandoned by God, and so that the field is left to the invasive force of evil. Because it is only the full presence of God that can remedy such trouble, the work of prayer is to voice a demanding, urgent summons that God should reengage the life of the speaker after a time of neglect and default. The issue, in such an exercise, is never a question about God's power, but it is about God's attentive fidelity from which God is said to have taken random sabbaticals, the kind of absences that Calvin never found necessary to acknowledge. It is clear that such a way of asserting the dynamics of God's presence constitutes a frontal refutation of Calvin's settlement of the matter.

Karl Barth, fully in the tradition of Calvin, struggles with the fullness of God's sovereignty vis à vis the capacity of human prayer to impact God. While of course confessing the sovereignty of God, Barth can make room for human impingement upon God: "Let us approach the subject from the given fact that God answers. God is not deaf, but listens; more than that, he acts. God does not act in the same way whether we pray or not. Prayer exerts an influence upon God's action, even upon his existence. This is what the word "answer" means."[11] Reflecting on Barth's astonishing phrasing in the *Church Dogmatics*, John Hesselink traces the way in which Barth continues to hold to a high, uncompromising view of God's sovereignty and yet allows for human partnership, so that human prayer as supplication has "impact with God."

> It turns out that Barth is more flexible and open than his critics give him credit for, although he will uphold steadfastly the sovereignty of God even in regard to prayer and providence. On the one hand, Barth does not hesitate

10. Ibid., 350.
11. Barth, *Prayer*, 13.

to say that God not only listens to our prayers, he acts
. . . Barth states the matter even more forcibly in his final
lectures . . . prayer "puts us in rapport with God and permits us to collaborate with him." Elsewhere Barth speaks of
Christians as "partners" with God in response to their calling
upon him in prayer . . . This kind of language has an Armin-
ian ring that is reinforced when Barth speaks elsewhere of a
"real cooperation" in doing God's will . . . In prayer, Christians enjoy "a genuine and actual share in the lordship of
God." However this is only one side of the matter. Thus far I
have deliberately omitted those passages where Barth speaks
out of the other side of his mouth.[12]

Barth takes care not to undo God's sovereignty; but this sovereign God, so Barth sees, also lets the faithful requests of his children
to be valued. The attempt of Barth so say both things, sovereignty
and human impact, allows for the dissonant piety of the Psalms,
a dynamism caught by Serene Jones. She reflects on the interface
between Karl Barth and Luce Irigaray, surely a strong foil for Barth.
She concludes in this way: ""What is clear, however, is that the God
confessed by each [Barth and Irigaray] is, contrary to traditional
metaphysics, a God who is not One but multiple, active and rela-
tional. And if this God is truly to meet humanity in a relationship
of mutuality, then this God must also be respected as incommen-
surably other, as a sign as well as an actual event of true alterity."[13]
The juxtaposition of "mutuality" and "incommensurability" is just
right. It is likely the case, however, that the abrasive self-declaration
of the Psalms on which Riemann meditates goes beyond what Barth
or Jones, along with Calvin, might readily intend.

By the time he finishes, Riemann judges that the voices sounded in the Psalter are "feisty" and have "room for *chutzpah*."[14] Such
freedom belongs to those who pray before God. It is clear that in its
sustained attempt to silence such a propensity to *chutzpah* and to
deny such emotions, the church has been, in its long vexed history,

12. Hesselink, "Karl Barth on Prayer," 84–85.

13. Jones, "This God which is Not One: Irigaray and Barth on the Divine,"
141.

14. See p. 60 below.

a wounding force for many people. In the interest of submissive reverence, it has required persons to be otherwise before God than they truly are. Thus the recurrence of this rhetoric, in all of its candid freedom, is treated as an unacceptable enterprise by those who would censor such daring public piety. Riemann's trenchant insight in this matter is a great gift, a gift that might be taken up even among systematic theologians who follow in the sake of Calvin. It will not do to blame Calvin too much for being a child of his time. But it will be an uncommon pity if some in the church now continue with Calvin's stance, as though we have learned nothing since Calvin, a view Calvin himself would have rejected. What we know is that pain honored in all its abrasiveness and outrageousness, when brought to speech, can be turned to positive energy. We know, moreover, that pain stifled and denied readily turns to violence. Calvin held to a stifling of such utterance, even when he found it voiced in the Psalms; such a stifling practice he thought, to the glory of God. Riemann shows that since the ancient wisdom and cunning of the Psalms, we have in fact always known better than that, even when we have lacked to courage to act so. The people who prayed (and continue to pray) these Psalms intended serious engagement before God with life as it truly is. Their utterances assume and advocate the truth, grounded in lived reality, that the God addressed in such prayers is likewise intending serious engagement. Such a recognition takes this cacophony of voices as a practice of the truth that makes free. We are greatly in Riemann's debt. We may take his study as an invitation to faith as daring as it is evidenced to be in this old book. We may still be learning "the right way"!

Walter Brueggemann
Columbia Theological Seminary

Acknowledgments

My sincere thanks to Herbert B. Huffmon, my friend and former colleague at Drew University, for his generous help and support in the project from the very start, and to Drew Theological Seminary, for inviting me to give the matriculation address in September 1987, in which these issues were first articulated. A more developed version was presented in August 1991, to the Colloquium for Biblical Research. I am especially grateful to Suzanne Selinger, who graciously read a later version and offered many helpful comments. I am indebted also to Louis Stulman and John Kaltner, who invited me to include this study in *Inspired Speech: Prophecy in the Ancient Near East. Essays in Honour of Herbert B. Huffmon* (London: T. & T. Clark, 2004), and to Walter Brueggemann, who suggested making it available in monograph form.

1

Introduction

SOME YEARS AGO ONE of Calvin's writings on prayer found its way into the syllabus for a course I taught on the book of Psalms. It was this work that provided the point of departure for the present study. What first drew my attention was his keen sense that many of the prayers of the Psalter do not follow his own guidelines for due and proper prayer, and his directness in saying so. This is a notably candid assessment, far less common in the interpretive tradition than it ought to be. In spite of all he was able to say in praise of the Psalter, when all was said and done he could not commend it to his readers as a book of model prayers they needed only to imitate. When he praised it he had other uses in mind, as we shall see. There is no doubt either that his judgment was correct; taken as a group, the prayer psalms[1] do not conform to his own convictions about the proprieties to be observed in prayer.

I have come to the conclusion that the piety implicit in the prayer psalms and the piety Calvin himself endorsed and espoused differ significantly. They embody fundamentally different perceptions of prayer, what it is, why one engages in it, what one hopes

1. By "prayer psalms" I refer to those biblical scholars classify as *Klagelieder* (in English current usage favors "complaint psalms" rather than "laments"; my own preference would be "plaint psalms"). There are more psalms of this type in the Psalter than of any other. They share many conventional elements; among those that are almost always present are plaint and petition.

to achieve by it. From what I have said thus far it may appear that this was also his view. It was not. The purpose of this study is to learn why it was not and to trace some of the more important consequences.

Calvin did not work in splendid isolation, to be sure. He was a figure of his time, his approach was shaped by the interests and conflicts of the period, and he was of course building upon the work of others. He was drawing upon the rich traditions of the ancient and medieval Church, and the work of other reformers who were his predecessors and contemporaries, Luther above all. In the case of the book of Psalms he was making use of many sources, and may well have been influenced by the commentary of Martin Bucer of Strassburg in particular.[2] He was well read in Augustine, whom he greatly revered, and the introspective character of Augustine's writings doubtless encouraged him in a reading of the Psalms in the same mode, even though the fourth-century bishop had no comparable interest in the Psalter's historical setting and Calvin is frequently critical of his exegetical judgment.[3] In view of recent studies that have shown how extensively scholars of this period drew upon their predecessors in the late Medieval period as well as each other, it cannot simply be assumed that he was solely responsible even for those insights that most shaped his understanding of Psalter piety.

For the purposes of the present study we shall focus our attention upon Calvin and his own historical setting, leaving aside the matter of antecedents and forerunners. The clarity of his thought

---

2. On Bucer's prolix but widely-read commentary see Hobbs (1984). Calvin refers to the commentaries of Bucer and Musculus in the preface to his commentary on the Psalms, 1557; Bucer's was published under his own name in 1554 (the first edition, under the pseudonym Aretius Felinus, in 1529), Musculus' in 1551; see Parker's comment in Calvin 1965: 11, 387 nn. 2, 3. By 1557 many such works had been published; the list of books on the Psalter provided by Hobbs (1990: 223–25) includes Latin works by nineteen authors published 1508–1546.

3. For example, "All this may be plausible, and, in its own place, useful, but [it] proceeds upon a complete misapprehension of the meaning of the passage" (*Com. Ps.* 58:1). Citations from the Psalms commentary, including Calvin's translations of the biblical text, are taken from the James Anderson edition for the Calvin Translation Society (1845–49).

makes it relatively easy to see what led him to take the stance he did and, more important, how he managed to work it out and justify it. There is at least a hint, as we shall see, that he did not do this all at once, that there was something about the Psalms he had to ponder for some time before he was willing to commit himself in writing. But at least by the time he published his commentary on the Psalms he had found a way to disapprove much that the psalmists say in their prayers and yet approve the piety to which they were ultimately committed. He regarded the piety that lay behind the Psalms as due and proper and, in all essential respects, compatible with his own. In the end it was no doubt precisely because he was so certain he recognized and approved their piety that he could so confidently fault them for their lapses, shortcomings and excesses, while identifying personally with their faith and their failings.

I shall take the Psalms as Calvin himself read them, and ask how he proceeded from that point to an understanding of their piety. Citations of the biblical text, for example, will follow his translation and stand for the most part without comment. It goes without saying that his judgments about text, translation, authorship and historical setting do not always conform to those of contemporary biblical scholarship, but it serves my purpose best to allow him his own perspective on these matters. His understanding of the piety of the prayer psalms does not hinge upon matters of this sort, and I suspect he would have held to this understanding even if he had known of, and accepted, the latest historical-critical judgments about them. That there are well-known scholars trained in the historical-critical method who espouse a similar understanding today shows well enough that it can be done.

2

Discerning a Savor of Intemperance

CALVIN'S DISQUIET WITH DAVID

CALVIN IS SPEAKING OF prayer in his *The Institutes of the Christian Religion* when he writes that "No one has ever carried this out with the uprightness that was due; for, not to mention the rank and file, how many complaints of David savor of intemperance!" (*Inst.* 3.20.16).[1] With these words he introduces an assessment of the psalms that tells us a great deal about his own understanding of their piety. To be sure, the premise that not even the prayers of biblical saints are wholly satisfactory follows from his basic theological stance. He uses David to clinch the argument precisely because he greatly admires "that most illustrious prince and prophet" and ranks him above all other psalmists. But there is a certain sense of amazement here that this "savor of intemperance" should be so prevalent and so obvious, and an implication that the reader must surely have felt this too.

"Not that he would either deliberately expostulate with God or clamor against his judgments," Calvin continues, "but that, fainting with weakness, he finds no other solace better than to cast his own sorrows into the bosom of God." He means to put the emphasis here

1. All quotations are from the McNeill-Battles edition (1960).

4

upon David's good intention and the mitigating circumstances; in such cases God is forgiving, and this is the point he has been aiming at all along. "God tolerates even our stammering and pardons our ignorance whenever something inadvertently escapes us; as indeed without this mercy there would be no freedom to pray."

At the same time Calvin's own disquiet comes through clearly enough. He must feel that David did sometimes "expostulate with God" and "clamor against his judgments" or he would not think it an adequate defense to say that David would not do either "deliberately." The sentence that follows has the same double edge. "But although David intended to submit completely to God's will, and prayed with no less patience than zeal to obtain his request, yet there come forth—sometimes, rather, boil up—turbulent emotions, quite out of harmony with the first rule we laid down."

A Work in Revision

As Calvin writes this he is nearing fifty and his health is deteriorating. Perhaps sensing that his time is short—he would die before he reached fifty-five—he has set himself to produce a new and final edition of his major work, adding here one of several wholly new sections to the chapter on prayer. He had been only twenty-six, and had not yet laid eyes on Geneva, when the first, much smaller edition was published as "an almost complete summary of piety" (so the 1536 title page).[2] At that time prayer was already the topic of one of the book's six chapters, so he has been thinking and writing about this for half his life.

The chapter had been revised and expanded soon after for the second edition of the *Institutes*, published in 1539, but it had hardly been touched since.[3] He is now thoroughly reworking it; by

2. See Battles' translation of the 1536 edition (Calvin 1975)

3. The 1559 edition of the chapter comprises some 2500 lines of text in the critical edition of Barth and Niesel (Calvin 1926–70: IV, 298–368). Of these, some 1200 lines have been carried over without change from the 1539 edition, including some 680 lines unchanged from the 1536 edition, much of it exposition of the Lord's Prayer as one would expect (*Inst.* 3.20.34–49+50). Some 285 lines are 1536/39 text now reedited for 1559. There is little text from

the time it is published in 1559 much of the text will be revised and more than a third will be entirely new.[4] What is surprising—and intriguing—is that the new text will triple the number of references to the Psalter.[5] It will also introduce general observations on the book, most of the references to David by name, and all of the critical remarks about the prayers of the psalmists.

One reason for this must certainly be that he had just recently published (in July 1557) a commentary on the book of Psalms, the fruit of some five years of study and teaching,[6] all of it undertaken

---

later editions: some 100 lines added in 1543 (including the whole of section 32, on church singing) and a mere half-dozen in the major edition of 1550. A relatively small part of the earlier text was not carried over into the 1559 edition, mainly in sections 12–15.

4. Of the approximately 2500 lines in Calvin's *Opera Selecta*, some 900 (36%) are entirely new text; some 285 lines (an additional 11%) are older text reedited.

5. Fifty-four references to thirty-six psalms were marked in the printed text of 1559. Six derive from the 1536 edition, and ten from the 1539 edition—together a total of sixteen references to twelve psalms. There are none in the brief sections of text from 1543 and 1550. When earlier text was not carried over in 1559 no references were lost. On this reckoning the 1559 edition added thirty-eight references (70% of the total) and drew upon twenty-four additional psalms (67% of the total). If we added two references marked in earlier editions, two marked in the 1561 printing, one marked in the French editions 1541sqq, and three more identified by Barth and Niesel in footnotes, the count would be sixty-two references to forty-two psalms. On this reckoning forty-one references were added in the 1559 edition (66% of the total), drawing upon twenty-seven additional psalms (64% of the total). On either reckoning there are more than four references per hundred lines in newly composed 1559 text, compared to just over one per hundred in text carried over from earlier editions. Granted that there are always uncertainties in determining what is a "reference," the pattern of distribution is so striking this hardly matters. While there are additional references to other biblical books also, none is really comparable; the largest additions are six each to Isaiah (to make nineteen), Jeremiah (to make eleven), the Synoptics (to make twenty-one), and James (to make twelve).

6. "I expounded the Book of Psalms in this small school of mine three years ago" (preface to the commentary, cited from Calvin 1965: 15). T. H. L. Parker concludes that this must refer to the lectures, conducted in Latin, which he gave sometime between 1552 and 1555 or 1556. Calvin had worked with the Psalms before; at least as early as 1545 he was preaching on them occasionally on Sunday afternoons. For details see Parker's comments in Calvin 1965: 5–6; see also Parker 1986: 30).

since the last major revision of the *Institutes*. In fact, the Friday afternoon *Congrégation*, a study group conducted in French that the Genevan pastors were required to attend and to which others came also, had been working through the book under Calvin's direction for several years and would continue to do so until August 1559, the very month the final edition of the *Institutes* was published.[7] Evidently the book of Psalms had come to play an increasingly prominent part in his thinking about prayer, perhaps precisely because of the problems it posed for him.

The Rules for Framing Proper Prayer

When he writes that David's complaints are "quite out of harmony with the first rule we laid down," he is referring to the rules "for framing prayer duly and properly," which he has just finished setting out in the first part of the chapter. To call them "rules" is perhaps a bit misleading; as François Wendel (1963: 254) remarks, "it is a question of the general attitude required of the faithful rather than of precise and clearly-distinguishable rules." Nevertheless, Calvin clearly means them to be taken seriously, and his presentation takes the form of a rather stern lecture on proper attitudes in prayer.

In the course of two decades they have grown from two rules to four, and here in the final edition he takes eleven sections to present them (more than sixteen pages in the McNeill-Battles translation), so they are not easily summarized. Calvin is brilliant, well-educated, eloquent, and thorough, but he lacks Luther's gift for the pithy phrase. Of necessity I offer them here in capsule form, but I shall use his own words as much as I can.

"Now . . . let this be the first rule: that we be disposed in mind and heart as befits those who enter conversation with God." The metaphor of conversation with divine majesty suggests two proprieties we must observe: to give God our undivided attention and to keep ourselves from shameful desires. Thus, "we are to rid ourselves of all alien and outside cares, by which the mind, itself a wanderer,"

---

7. On the *Congrégation*, see Parker (1986: 14–15). The group had begun its study of the book of Psalms in 1555.

is so easily distracted (*Inst.* 3.20.4). The newly added text puts this categorically: "Let us therefore realize that the only persons who duly and properly gird themselves to pray are those who are so moved by God's majesty that they come to it freed from earthly cares and affections" (*Inst.* 3.20.5). The same consideration requires that there "enter our hearts no desire and no wish at all of which we should be ashamed to make him a witness (*Inst.* 3.20.3)." Instead, we must "rise to a purity worthy of God" (*Inst.* 3.20.4).

The first rule has a complement that is almost an additional rule: "not to ask any more than God allows" (*Inst.* 3.20.5), but rather to "submit completely to God's will" (*Inst.* 3.20.16). And we have not been left to wonder what God wills for us; it is what God has promised in the Scriptures. It follows that "where no certain promise shows itself, we must ask of God conditionally" (*Inst.* 3.20.15), which is to say, we must add "if it be thy will" or "nevertheless, thy will be done."

"Let this be the second rule: that in our petitions we ever sense our own insufficiency, and earnestly pondering how [much] we need all we seek, join with this prayer an earnest—nay, burning—desire to attain it" (*Inst.* 3.20.6).

The third rule is to repent, and in a sense this comes first. "Lawful prayer . . . demands repentance . . . Let each one, therefore, as he prepares to pray be displeased with his own evil deeds, and (something that cannot happen without repentance) let him take the person and disposition of a beggar" (*Inst.* 3.20.7). "The beginning, and even the preparation, of proper prayer is the plea for pardon with a humble and sincere confession of guilt," for God cannot "chance to be propitious to any but those whom he has pardoned" (*Inst.* 3.20.9).

"The fourth rule is that, thus cast down and overcome by true humility, we should be nonetheless encouraged to pray by a sure hope that our prayer will be answered" (*Inst.* 3.20.11). Indeed, "only that prayer is acceptable to God which is born, if I may so express it, out of such presumption of faith, and is grounded in unshaken assurance of hope" (*Inst.* 3.20.12). It is Christ himself who "calls this principle to the attention of all of us with this saying, 'I say unto you, whatever you seek . . . believe that you will receive it, and it will come to you'" (Mark 11:24). Prayers that lack this are irritating: "It is amazing how much our lack of trust provokes God if we request of him a boon that we do not expect" (*Inst.* 3.20.11).

Even before he has finished the first rule, Calvin warns this will not be easy. "Because our abilities are far from able to match such perfection, we must seek a remedy to help us." It is for this reason "God gives us the Spirit as our teacher in prayer, to tell us what is right and temper our emotions." (The "tempering of the emotions" is a prominent theme in Calvin's piety, and we shall return to it.) But we must not presume upon this divine aid. "These things are not said in order that we, favoring our own slothfulness, may give over the function of prayer to the Spirit of God, and vegetate in that carelessness to which we are all too prone," for in this matter "God's will is to test how effectually faith moves in our hearts" (*Inst.* 3.20.5).

Bringing the Rules to the Psalms

These are the four rules Calvin has in mind as he reflects on David and the Psalter. They require reverence, submission to the will of God, earnest desire, humble penitence, and unwavering faith. Even though he places his own distinctive construction on several of these elements, as we shall see, the essential piety they describe has already had a long history and is certainly not his own invention.

When he proceeds to judge the Psalms by these rules he faces something of a problem. He is too able a biblical scholar to suppose they describe the way the psalmists actually frame their prayers, and yet he cannot imagine that the psalmists were indifferent to them or that the Holy Spirit was nodding. This is a particularly important matter, for his whole understanding of psalm piety is fundamentally shaped by the way he resolves this tension: *it appears self-evident to him that the psalmists intended to follow the rules he has set forth, but often failed to do so for very human reasons we must not approve but can readily understand.*

Seen in this light, the Psalms serve to confirm the judgment that prompts him to promulgate rules in the first place. Rules are needed because it does not come to us naturally and spontaneously to frame our prayers aright; on the contrary, due and proper prayer is a "goal not immediately attainable" toward which we must continually and earnestly strive. On this understanding he is able to turn even David's shortcomings and excesses to advantage; they reinforce his own theology of prayer rather than subvert it. The "savor of intemperance" in his complaints assures us that God will graciously tolerate and pardon our own ignorance and stammering, and at the same time warns us against carelessly, much less deliberately, praying the same way ourselves.

This inevitably shapes his understanding of the psalms as Holy Scripture. Even though the book of Psalms is inspired by the Holy Spirit, we are not to regard all it contains as exemplary prayer. The book is a record of the long-standing struggle to frame prayers rightly, not a sample-book of unblemished prayers that we can safely imitate. Many psalms represent the way believers do pray, rather than the way they ought to pray. And this is what the Holy Spirit intended in providing such forms of prayer for our instruction. Rather than copying them, we must learn from them not to be too quickly satisfied with our own efforts or too quickly disheartened when we fall short of the goal ourselves.

The correlate is that the rules for proper prayer are not, indeed cannot be, derived from the book of Psalms itself, since the book exhibits them only imperfectly. They must be discovered elsewhere and then applied to the psalms, just as Calvin is doing. This may, of course, involve us in judging the psalmists by a standard they did not intend to follow and would not even have recognized.

A straightforward comparative study, looking only for similarities and differences and not intending to make judgments about what is proper and what is not, might choose to bracket the issue entirely. It could bring together any collection of prayer texts (the Psalter, or a prayer book perhaps) and any protocol of prayer (even from a non-Judeo-Christian tradition) and ask to what extent they correlate. But even here one would certainly want to ask whether a different protocol is implicit in the text, if only to guard against possible misunderstandings.

Calvin has no such limited objective in mind. The piety he has tried to summarize in a few helpful rules is not one of many equally legitimate ways to frame prayer; it is the form of prayer that God both invites and commands us to use, authorized by Scripture and to be observed throughout the Church, and so he cannot avoid making judgments about the propriety of prayers in the Psalter and their implicit piety.

At the same time, he cannot simply bracket the question of the psalmists' own sense of propriety either, for he brings a self-consciously historical interest to the psalms, even if that is not his sole concern. As a scholar exercised in the New Learning, he wants to understand the psalms on their own terms, as ancient prayers occasioned by real circumstances in the lives of real people. But the intuition that allows him to bring theological conviction and historical interest together so easily—namely, that the psalmists share his own sense of what is right and are trying as best they can to follow it—succeeds rather too well, for it effectively silences the psalms as witnesses to their own intention. If it should happen that this intuition is wrong and the psalms have quite a different sense of what is proper in prayer, he has made it virtually impossible for them to tell him so. Whatever they say or do, he will have little difficulty accounting for it on his own terms.

Measuring the Psalms against the Rules

It is in the new text Calvin is composing for the 1559 edition, and especially in three wholly new sections he is adding to his account of the four rules, that he reflects on the negative between his rules and the psalms. In the first (*Inst.* 3.20.9), he is expanding on the third rule, to repent, which he has just introduced in the preceding section. Having said that "the plea for pardon with a humble and sincere confession of guilt" is "the beginning, and even the preparation, of proper prayer," he turns to the Psalter to demonstrate this. "Accordingly, it is no wonder if believers open for themselves the door to prayer with this key, as we learn from numerous passages of the Psalms," and he cites Psalms 25 and 51 as examples.

He has noticed that penitential statements of this sort are often lacking in biblical prayers, and he mentions this, but as a matter of no real consequence. "But even though the saints do not always beg forgiveness of sins in so many words, if we diligently ponder their prayers that Scripture relates" we will readily see "that they have received their intention to pray from God's mercy alone, and thus always have begun with appeasing him" (*Inst.* 3.20.9). Here he seems to lean over backwards to reconcile the psalms with a rule, not by chance the rule he regards as indispensable. It is doubtful he would be as generous with non-biblical prayers that did not "beg forgiveness in so many words" and whose penitential intent could be discovered only by diligent pondering.

The two other new sections (*Inst.* 3.20.15–16) come after he has finished setting out the rules and reflect on them as a set. The first begins "Here more than one question is raised: for Scripture relates that God has granted fulfillment of certain prayers," even though they were "not framed to the rule of the Word." He then discusses a number of biblical examples. One in particular shows how far he is willing to carry his critical assessment of the psalms: "And one psalm clearly teaches that prayers which do not reach heaven by faith still are not without effect," for it "lumps together those prayers which, out of natural feeling, necessity wrings from unbelievers just as much as from believers, yet from the outcome it proves that God is gracious toward them" (Psalm 107). Such divine gentleness does not, however, attest that God finds such prayers acceptable. "Nay, it is by this circumstance to emphasize or illumine his mercy whenever the prayers of unbelievers are not denied to them; and again to incite his true worshippers to pray the more, when they see that even ungodly wailings sometimes do some good" (*Inst.* 3.20.15).

The same note of cautious encouragement opens the new section that immediately follows: "This also is worth noting: what I have set forth on the four rules of right praying is not so rigorously required that God will reject those prayers in which he finds neither perfect faith nor repentance, together with a warmth of zeal and petitions rightly conceived." He then proceeds to measure the prayers of the saints against each of the rules in turn, drawing the lessons appropriate to proper piety.

With respect to the first rule, he begins as we have already noted: in many of David's complaints there are intemperate and turbulent emotions "quite out of harmony with the first rule that we laid down." As a particularly striking example he offers the way David ends the thirty-ninth psalm. "'Let me alone,' he says, 'before I depart, and be no more.' One might say that this desperate man seeks nothing except to rot in his evils, with God's hand withdrawn." It is obvious that "this holy man" is so carried away by violent sorrow that "he cannot control himself." But this is not an uncommon failing. In those trials also there are often uttered petitions not sufficiently consonant with the rule of God's Word, and in which the saints do not sufficiently weigh what is lawful and expedient." Whatever the extenuating circumstances, however, "all prayers marred by these defects deserve to be repudiated." And there is only one remedy: "provided the saints bemoan their sins, chastise themselves, and immediately return to themselves, God pardons them" (*Inst.* 3.20.16).

He finds they "likewise sin with regard to the second rule [keenly to sense our great need]; for they must repeatedly wrestle with their own coldness, and their need and misery do not sharply enough urge them to pray earnestly." As a result, "it often happens that their minds slip away and well-nigh vanish; accordingly, in this respect there is also need for pardon, lest our languid or mutilated, or interrupted and vague, prayers suffer a refusal" (*Inst.* 3.20.16).

Since he has already satisfied himself (in section 9) that biblical prayers always begin by appeasing God even though they "do not always beg forgiveness of sins in so many words," he does not fault the psalms with respect to the third rule (to repent). Instead, he cites David as a worthy example. "Although no believers neglect this topic"—for him this is a matter of definition, for they would not be believers if they did—"yet those truly versed in prayers know that they do not offer a tenth part of that sacrifice of which David speaks: 'The sacrifice acceptable to God is a broken spirit . . .'" (*Inst.* 3.20.16, citing Ps 51:17).

He is speaking of the fourth rule (that we pray in the unshakable faith that our prayer will be granted) when he writes: "Most of all it is weakness or imperfection of faith that vitiates believers' prayers, unless God's mercy succor them." He adds, "but no wonder God pardons this defect, since he often tests his own with sharp trials, as if he deliberately willed to snuff out their faith." To be "compelled to cry out, 'How long wilt thou be angry with the prayer of thy servant?' as if prayers themselves annoyed God," as Ps 80:4 does, is the hardest trial of all. "Innumerable examples of this kind occur in Scripture, from which it is clear the faith of the saints was often so mixed and troubled with doubts that in believing and hoping they yet betrayed some want of faith." But once again he ends with admonition. "I do not recount these matters in order that believers may confidently pardon themselves for anything but that by severely chastising themselves they may strive to overcome these obstacles." They should feel the depths of evil, "seeing that there is no prayer which in justice God would not loathe if he did not overlook the spots with which all are sprinkled." And yet in spite of Satan's efforts "they should nonetheless break through, surely persuaded that, although not freed of all hindrances, their efforts still please God and their petitions are approved, provided they endeavor and strive toward a goal not immediately attainable" (*Inst.* 3.20.16).

CALVIN'S APPROACH TO PSALM PIETY

Before we leave Calvin's chapter on prayer, there are four interrelated matters to which we should give particular attention: the locus of his concern, the theological stance he is bringing to his reading, the manner in which he accounts for the psalmists' lapses and excesses, and the emphasis he lays upon prayer as an introspective discipline.

The Locus of Concern

Precisely because he has presented the excesses and shortcomings of biblical prayer in his customary thorough way, it is worth noting that he has not even mentioned a topic some would put high on the list, namely, the attitude the psalmists take toward their enemies.8 In fact he will not refer to it anywhere in this chapter.

When he comes, later in the chapter, to the first two petitions of the Lord's Prayer (*Inst.* 3.20.41–42) he will speak of vengeance and the desire for the destruction of the wicked, but he will do so without mentioning the psalms. However much this aspect of the Psalter may trouble others, he does not consider it to be one of the psalmists' failings. (How he dealt with it will appear shortly, when we come to consider his commentary on the Psalms.)

It is something else that arouses his interest and concern, namely, the attitude the psalmists seem to take toward themselves and toward God. This is where they appear to depart most dramatically from the theology and piety with which he himself identifies and which he urges upon his readers. If we are to understand his approach to psalm piety, we must consider at least briefly the theological stance, by now well worked out and widely published, which his rules for right prayer presuppose.

The Theological Stance Brought to the Psalms

Earlier in the same book of the *Institutes* Calvin devotes an entire chapter to self-denial, which he calls the sum of the Christian life. This is at the heart of his appeals to submit totally to whatever God wills, and it leaves no room at all for complaints against God. Those who duly deny themselves will not "break forth into impatience and expostulate with God" even when they are ill and in terrible pain, because they know it to be ordained of God (*Inst.* 3.7.10). It is no surprise, then, that he prefers to believe that David did not reprove God deliberately.

---

8. Even Claus Westermann, who has written so much in appreciation of the biblical lament tradition and proposed reintroducing it in the Church, has reservations at this point. "For side by side with some of the psalms, which are among the most beautiful and profound in the Psalter and which we can use in our own prayers, as if they had been written with us in view, there are others of which we are forced to ask whether as Christians we really can recite and pray them, because of the imprecations against the psalmist's enemies" (1989: 65).

He also rationalizes the common biblical idiom that speaks of God in human terms. This is not a new interpretive strategy by any means, but it is particularly important to him—few things frighten him more than the thought that human beings might underestimate the gulf between themselves and Almighty God. The idiom is the way God "accommodates himself to the ordinary way of speaking on account of our ignorance, and sometimes, if I may be allowed the expression, stammers" (*Com. John* 3:12).[9] As a result, we must not be misled by biblical representations of God's moods or mental activities: "God, in punishing, has (according to our notion) the *appearance* of one in wrath. It signifies . . . *no such emotion* in God, but only has a reference to the perception and feeling of the sinner who is punished (*Com. Rom.* 1:18 [emphasis added])." The same is true of God's repenting of a decision, or God's grief (Dowey 1952: 243). The position is developed with great care and subtlety, but there is no mistaking its essential thrust.[10] It cannot help but shape his reading of the psalms, where such language is common coin.

But if we must never object or complain, and God's decisions are always for the best and cannot be changed, what can be the purpose of petitioning God in prayer? Is it even appropriate to do so? In good rhetorical fashion he readily acknowledges the problem,

---

9. Citations from Calvin's commentaries cite the translations of the Calvin Translation Society's edition (Edinburgh, 1843–55). T. H. L. Parker's revised translation of his commentary on Psalms 1–33 (Calvin 1965), which draws upon the 1571 translation by Arthur Golding, is cited only for Calvin's letter "To the godly Readers." The passages from Calvin's *Com. John* are cited by Dowey 1952: 243. Cf. *Inst.* 1.13.1 (text from 1539): "The Anthropomorphites . . . are easily refuted. For who even of slight intelligence does not understand that, as nurses commonly do with infants, God is wont in a measure to 'lisp' in speaking to us? Thus such forms of speaking do not so much express clearly what God is like as accommodate the knowledge of him to our slight capacity. To do this he must descend far beneath his loftiness."

10. Dowey offers a more careful statement than I am able to present here, distinguishing the ways Calvin treats three different levels of metaphorical language about God (1952: 243–44). It is worth noting that when Calvin writes about prayer and the Psalms, he is by and large content to employ the biblical idiom himself (there is of course a long tradition for this). But we realize that he has not forgotten it is God's accommodation to us as soon as he begins to explain the purpose of prayer and offer his four rules.

and puts the question to himself early in the chapter on prayer: "But, someone will say, does God not know, even without being reminded, both in what respect we are troubled and what is expedient for us, so that it may seem in a sense superfluous that he should be stirred up by our prayers . . . ?" (*Inst.* 3.20.3). His answer is that people who reason this way do not observe the purpose God had in mind. "He ordained it not so much for his own sake as for ours." In fact it is "for God's sake" only in one respect: God commands that we pray. "He wills—as is right—that his due be rendered to him." But prayers do not move God, or change God's attitude, or alter in any way what God has decreed from all eternity. It is we who are changed by the discipline of prayer, by which the Holy Spirit schools us in proper attitudes "in mind and heart" (*Inst.* 3.20.4).[11]

All three of these concerns come together here. Prayer itself is a form of divine accommodation, and the discipline of prayer leads to self-denial. But it is the last point—that prayer is meant to have its effect upon us rather than upon God—which particularly shapes his reading of the Psalms. If he is more articulate and categorical about this than many have been, he at least puts the issue clearly and does not shy from what is, after all, one of the really profound theological puzzles: how to reconcile the practice of prayer with the doctrine that God is omnipotent, omniscient, omnipresent, impassible, and unchanging.

Accounting for the Psalmists' Lapses

Calvin takes it for granted that in at least all these essentials there is no contradiction between the psalmists' perception of God and his own. That is why it appears self-evident to him that they intend to follow the rules he sets forth, even if they do not always succeed. But these departures are by no means rare, as he recognizes;

11. Cf. the list of six benefits of prayer in *Inst.* 3.20.3: through prayer we learn to seek God with a burning desire, become accustomed to flee to God in every need, bridle our emotions and purify our desires, prepare ourselves to receive God's gifts with gratitude, embrace what we receive with greater delight, meditate more ardently on God's kindness, and finally confirm God's providence.

in psalms of petition they occur more often than not. How is this to be explained? Ultimately by human depravity, to be sure, but if that is all there is to it the psalmists have more claim to our sympathy than to our respect.

As we have seen, Calvin's view is that David's complaints savor of intemperance because he was "fainting with weakness"; he utters petitions "not sufficiently consonant with the rule of God's Word" because he is desperate, carried away by violent sorrow, and cannot control himself. And this is not uncommon; the saints often fall into this error when they are similarly tried. When their faith is often "so mixed and troubled with doubts" that even in their believing and hoping they betray "some want of faith," this is also a result of the sharp trials they have been made to suffer.

In short, Calvin ascribes these defects in large part to the extremity of the psalmists' situation. David would not have prayed like this if he had been in his right mind. He must be beside himself, overwhelmed by misery and trouble, in such desperate straits that he can no longer give thought to the proprieties of prayer which he would otherwise have been careful to observe.

When the psalmists describe their situation to God, they tend to speak in the direst terms. They present themselves as miserable, bereft of friends, surrounded by gloating and malicious enemies, falsely accused and persecuted, close to death, and very nearly despairing. No one, not even God, is coming to their aid. The strategy is pervasive and the language highly conventional, and one might well suspect it is heightened speech calculated to draw God's attention and pity, but we would not expect Calvin to allow for this, and he does not. He pictures their situation precisely as they describe it, and he understandably feels that anyone committed, as he is and as they must surely be, to reverent, restrained, submissive and undoubting prayer would find it difficult to keep to such a form in these overwhelming circumstances.

He finds the argument so persuasive he can even turn it around and infer the extremity of the psalmists' circumstances from the fact that their prayers depart from the proper form. Note his comment, "Now, as a man, who is distinguished by courage, does not cry out and complain, and as we know that David did not shrink in bearing his afflictions, we may gather from this, that his sufferings were severe and painful in the extreme, inasmuch as he not only wept bitterly, but was also forced to cry out and complain" (*Com. Ps.* 38:8).

At this point I wish only to observe that, whatever one decides about the psalmists' actual circumstances, it is rather bold to suggest that they pray as they do only because they have been driven to it.[12] Granted that desperate people may utter unseemly prayers, heedless of their own avowed piety, it is still difficult to imagine that any religious community would survive very long if this became the general practice, or that it would develop a conventional form for such prayers, as the psalmists have done. It is equally hard to imagine that a religious community would cherish and preserve such prayers, let alone gather more psalms of this genre than any other into its sacred book of collected psalms. But now I am raising questions it would never have occurred to Calvin to ask, and anticipating a discussion to follow later in the study. For the moment it is sufficient to point out that by "defending" the psalmists in this way he is effectively securing a place for his own piety.

Prayer as an Introspective Discipline

If the extremity of the psalmists' circumstances helps to explain the excesses and shortcomings of their prayers, it follows that we

---

12. A supposition often made by modern scholars to account for plaint psalms which make accusations against God follows the same line of reasoning and is open to the same objection. Namely, that these psalms can only be a response to a profound "crisis of faith" and therefore probably derive from a period of great national calamity (most often proposed: the sixth century BCE following the conquest of Jerusalem and the deportations to Babylonia). The same may be said of Westermann's attempt to account for "what is said concerning the enemy" in the plaint psalms of the individual: "What can be seen reflected in them . . . is the phenomenon of the gradual disintegration and decline of the community in which antagonisms (which we are no longer able to discern in detail) become simply overwhelming" (1981: 194). It is often the case that biblical scholars appeal to the social context to account for aspects of biblical culture they do not approve; they are less likely to do so for aspects which have their endorsement.

cannot use these prayers as models without taking their special situation into account. Calvin, as we would expect, draws just this conclusion. As he says of Ps 25:6, "This form of prayer cannot be used with propriety, unless when God is hiding his face from us, and seems to take no interest at all in us" (*Com. Ps.* 25:6).

He is less concerned to make the point that grave misfortunes may sometimes account for extraordinary biblical prayers, however, than to urge that they should always move us to pray: "for the saints the occasion that best stimulates them to call upon God is when, distressed by their own need, they are troubled by the greatest unrest, and are almost driven out of their senses, until faith opportunely comes to their relief" (*Inst.* 3.20.11). Indeed, God may send troubles for this very reason. "On account of these things, our most merciful Father . . . very often gives the impression of one sleeping or idling in order that he may train us, otherwise idle and lazy, to seek, ask, and entreat him to our great good" (*Inst.* 3.20.3). In fact, "the more harshly troubles, discomforts, fears, and trials of other sorts press us, the freer is our access to him, as if God were summoning us to himself" (*Inst.* 3.20.7).

All this serves to direct our attention inwardly, away from the troubles we suffer and toward the way we are responding to them. The gravest misfortune would be no obstacle if there were sufficient faith, and God may allow it precisely as a trial of faith. The real conflict takes place within us, and it has its roots in our carnal and fallen nature. The rules themselves reflect this by giving such close attention to the inner state of the one who is praying: "As we must turn keenness of mind toward God, so affection of heart has to follow" (*Inst.* 3.20.5).

But this inner striving has two aspects, well illustrated in the same paragraph by the dual role of the Holy Spirit, who "rouses in us assurance, desires, and sighs, to conceive which our natural powers would scarcely suffice," and who is at the same time "our teacher in prayer, to tell us what is right [in prayer] and temper our emotions" (*Inst.* 3.20.5). Behind the Spirit's double role lies the conviction that there are two "temptations" in particular against which all believers must constantly struggle "when they groan with weariness under the weight of present ills, and also are troubled and tormented by the fear of greater ones" (*Inst.* 3.20.11). One is to feel so despondent they come to be discouraged and lose their confidence, hope, ardor, and incentive. The other is to feel so frantic and overwrought they come to be carried away by their emotions and lose their patience, humility, reverence, and self-control. The "goal not immediately attainable" is to bring these extremes under control by faith, self-discipline, and moderation.

This is, after all, what the rules are framed to promote, and the central place they give to right attitudes requires that those who pray be constantly monitoring their inmost thoughts, feelings, desires and motivations for any deviation from what is due and proper. This is a decidedly controlled and introspective mode of prayer, self-reflective, self-yielding, self-denying, self-accusing, and self-correcting. It is intensely inward-looking even if it is not self-induced or self-empowered, but wholly owing, as Calvin insists, to the grace of God and the working of the Holy Spirit.

Calvin is certainly neither the first nor the last to espouse this mode of prayer or to bring it to his reading of the Psalms. I do not doubt that it has its own warrant as a form of piety, but whether assuming it for the psalms allows the voice of the psalmists themselves to be heard is another matter altogether.

3

Unfolding the Inmost
Feelings of David

THE COMMENTARY ON THE BOOK OF PSALMS

THE MASSIVE COMMENTARY ON the Psalms, which Calvin brought
to print in July 1557, helps to account for the remarkable increase
in psalm references in the chapter on prayer in the final (1559)
edition of *The Institutes of the Christian Religion*. It appears that
the commentary had a similar impact upon the 1559 Institutes as
a whole, for there is a striking increase in psalm references in each
of the four books.[1]

Few of the new 1559 references outside *Institutes* 3.20 are concerned with the piety of David and the psalmists, and those which
are add nothing to what Calvin says in the chapter on prayer. If
anyone should doubt, however, that he has carefully considered
the stance he takes toward psalm piety in this chapter, these few
passages scattered through the other books offer some measure of
assurance on the point.

---

1. By a rough calculation, new and edited text adds something on the order
of 240–270 psalm references to make a total of 510 or so; i.e., about half were
evidently introduced in 1559.

But it is the commentary itself that is decisive. Here Calvin has more space to develop his ideas, and the commentary format itself requires him to deal with each psalm in turn. As we now proceed to examine it, our interest is to discover whether the approach Calvin takes to the piety of David and the other psalmists anticipates the one he will take in the *Institutes*, and to see how he elaborates it.

The Genesis of the Work

It is worth noting at the outset that we have uncommonly direct access to Calvin's exegesis of the Psalms, for he wrote the manuscript for the commentary himself. Among all his Old Testament commentaries, this was the first of only three to be produced this way— "the three commentaries proper," as T. H. L. Parker terms them.[2] The majority were transcripts of his lectures, taken down by others, and prepared for publication under his general supervision. "His oversight of the material was in no way a revision. He left in the many involutions, repetitions, and asides which a revision would have excised" (Parker 1986: 28).

In this case he had refused to permit the publication of transcripts, even though others had begun early in the course to record the lectures for this purpose.[3] He had resolved, he says, "not to publish more extensively what I had uttered familiarly to those of my own household" (Calvin 1965: 15). Martin Bucer's "singular learning . . . had at least wrought this effect, that there was the less necessity for my work," and soon after, the commentaries of Wolfgang Musculus were before the public also. When he comes to explain why he had at last allowed himself to be prevailed upon, he reports

2. The others are the Mosaic, published in 1563, and Joshua, published the following year (Parker 1986: 29–33).

3. The earlier commentaries on Isaiah (1551) and Genesis (1554) had been produced from transcripts taken by his secretary, Nicholas des Gallars. The commentary on Hosea, published the same year as the commentary on the Psalms (1557), had been transcribed by three secretaries from notes they had taken. In a letter dated June 16, 1555, des Gallars had offered to send Calvin "what I took down from your lectures on the Psalms of David . . . if they can be of any use to you or lighten your task at all." See Parker 1986: 24–31.

that he had "one reason for obeying them . . . and that was, lest at any time what had been taken down from my discourses, should be brought out without my consent or knowledge"; he had been "driven by this fear, rather than led by my own free will to weave this web" (Calvin 1965: 15).

Why had he been so reluctant? According to Parker (1986: 30), "quite simply they [the lecture transcripts] were below the standards he set himself." But in this case I suspect there was an additional factor, an uneasiness about reconciling the psalms with his own sense of proper prayer. The way he describes his experience suggests that it was not sub-standard transcripts, but an uncertainty about finding the right words, which was holding him back; the turning point came when "suddenly, contrary to my purpose (I know not by what impulse), I made a trial of a Latin exposition in one Psalm." Encouraged that his success, "while it answered my wishes, far surpassed my hopes," he "began to attempt the same in some few others," and "as the work proceeded, I began more distinctly to perceive how far from superfluous this labour would be' (Calvin 1965: 15–16). If the task of reconciling the psalms with his own piety had given him trouble before, the problem was now resolved.

The Commentary and the Chapter on Prayer

Our first question is readily answered. The stance he takes toward psalm piety in this earlier work is essentially the same as in the chapter on prayer in the *Institutes*. Some points stand out because they are so often repeated, and a number are discussed in much greater detail. Prayers for vengeance, which were passed over in the chapter on prayer, receive a good deal of attention here. We will return to these and other matters shortly; the first task is to set out the essential similarity.

The rules for right prayer are implicit throughout, everywhere guiding his reading. He does not offer them as a set, as he does in the chapter on prayer, but when he alludes to them he employs virtually the same language. For example: "We are to hold this as a general rule in seeking to conciliate God, that we must pray for the pardon of our sins" (*Com. Ps.* 143:2). Or again: "And this is the rule which ought to be observed by us in our prayers; we should in everything conform our requests to the divine will, as John also instructs us (1 John v:14). And, indeed, we can never pray in faith unless we attend, in the first place, to what God commands, that our minds may not rashly and at random start aside in desiring more than we are permitted to desire and pray for" (*Com. Ps.* 7:6).

He has no doubt that the psalmists are deeply concerned about right attitudes and carefully monitoring them, just as the rules urge all the faithful to be. By saying, "My God! My God!" David "keeps all his thoughts and feelings under restraint, that they may not break beyond due bounds" (*Com. Ps.* 22:1). Commenting on the verse "Make me to know thy ways," he writes that he has "no hesitation in referring the prayer" to the circumstance that David is "afraid of yielding to the feeling of impatience, or the desire of revenge, or some extravagant and unlawful impulse" (*Com. Ps.* 25:4). We noted earlier his warning on the opening of Psalm 102: "No person could utter these words with the mouth without profaning the name of God, unless he were, at the same time, actuated by a sincere and earnest affection of heart" (*Com. Ps.* 102:1–2).

As the last citation already indicates, he finds passages that alarm him. His response to the cry in Psalm 25, "Remember, O Jehovah! thy tender mercies," is to say "From this it appears . . . that David . . . had lost all sense of God's mercy; for he calls upon God to remember for him his favor, in such a manner as if he had already forgotten it" (*Com. Ps.* 25:6). In Psalm 39 he notes "a kind of irony" in the petition "O Jehovah! cause me to know my end"; it is "not without anger and resentment that David speaks in this manner," and "seeing he finds fault with God," he exceeds what is proper (*Com. Ps.* 39:4). The reference in Psalm 88 to "the slain who lie in the grave, whom thou rememberest no more" he ascribes to a psalmist who "spoke less advisedly than he ought to have done" and allowed "unadvised words to escape from his lips" (*Com. Ps.* 88:5).

Just as he does in the chapter on prayer, however, he pleads extenuating circumstances:

"[T]he complaints of the people of God ought not to be judged of according to a perfect rule, because they proceed not from a settled and an undisturbed state of mind, but have always some excess arising from the impetuosity or vehemence of the affections at work in their minds" (*Com. Ps.* 89:47).

To return to the examples above, it appears to him from Ps 25:6 "that David was grievously afflicted and tried," and from Ps 39:4–6 "that David was transported by an improper and sinful excess of passion" and "spoke under the influence of a distempered and troubled state of mind." As for Ps 88:5, he is sure the psalmist knew well enough "that the dead are under the divine protection," but being "as it were, so stunned and stupefied when sorrow overmastered him," he spoke unadvisedly "in the first paroxysm of his grief."

It is important to Calvin that the psalmists are quick to correct such faults themselves. "There will occasionally escape from the lips of a saint, when he prays, some complaining exclamations which cannot be altogether justified, but he soon recalls himself to the exercise of believing supplication" (*Com. Ps.* 55:9). Thus while the psalmist who calls upon God to "arise" and "forget not the poor" in Ps 10:12 has fallen into the very error he has just condemned in others, "he proceeds at once to correct it, and resolutely struggles with himself, and restrains his mind from forming such conceptions of God, as would reflect dishonor upon his righteousness and glory" (*Com. Ps.* 10:12; he finds the correction in verse 14, "Thou hast seen it; for thou considerest mischief . . ."). In Psalm 30, by crying "Hear, O Jehovah! and have mercy upon me" (v. 10), David "softens and corrects his former complaint; for it would have been absurd to expostulate with God like one who despaired of safety [as the psalmist had done in v. 9], and to leave off in this fretful temper" (*Com. Ps.* 30:10).

We may judge how keenly he feels the need for this self-correction by his eagerness to find examples of it. Having criticized David for finding fault with God in Ps 39:4–6, he takes comfort that David implores God's mercy "a little after, having corrected himself; for he does not continue to indulge in rash and inconsiderate lamentations, but lifting up his soul in the exercise of faith, he attains heavenly consolation" (*Com. Ps.* 39:6). By his own account, however, the last verse of the psalm "indicates the feeling almost of despair" (*Com. Ps.* 39.13). In the course of his exposition of Psalm 89 he remarks that "we shall afterwards see that the prophet, when he blesses God at the close of the psalm, affords a proof of tranquil submission, by which he corrects or qualifies his complaints" (*Com. Ps.* 89:38). But it takes a good deal of imagination to read "tranquil submission" into v. 52, even if one were to accept that it is the last verse of the psalm rather than one of the conventional blessings that bring books one through four of the Psalter to a close. Calvin insists it is not a concluding blessing, but his counter-argument— "as if the language of praise and thanksgiving to God were not as suitable at the close of a psalm as at the opening of it"—misses the point entirely.[4]

FOUR MATTERS OF PARTICULAR INTEREST

I turn now to several matters which receive particular attention in the commentary. All of them have to do with the means and ends of prayer. For convenience of presentation I have grouped them under four headings: praying for pardon, to motivate God, to motivate oneself, and for vengeance. Taken together they will serve to give a fully rounded view of Calvin's understanding of the prayer psalms. In many respects they will again show continuity with the 1559 revision of the chapter on prayer in his *Institutes*. But they will also indicate that he had recognized features of prayer in the Psalter which he did not choose to mention in this chapter or recommend to his "Godly Readers" in the 1557 preface to his commentary on Psalms.

---

4. Although he does not regard any of these verses (Ps 41:13 [Heb. 14]; 72:19 [Heb. 20]; 89:52 [Heb. 53]; 106:48) as blessings which conclude a book, he acknowledges that "some interpreters" say this of Ps 89:52, and (in this case only) "readily" grants it is true of the last words of the verse ("Amen and amen").

Praying for Pardon

It comes as no surprise that Calvin is as emphatic about the need for repentance as he is in the chapter on prayer, and he puts it in almost identical language: "It is indeed true, in general, that men pray in a wrong way, and in vain, unless they begin by seeking the forgiveness of their sins . . . The right and proper order of prayer therefore is, as I have said, to ask, at the very outset, that God would pardon our sins" (*Com. Ps.* 25:7). And he is no less certain that the psalmists observed this order. Of David he asserts categorically that "in his sickness, as in all his other adversities, David views the hand of God lifted up to punish him for his sins" (*Com. Ps.* 38:2).

At the same time he sees no reason to go out of his way to make a case for this. He is content to claim any allusion to guilt as support (e.g., Ps 25:7), and, when he encounters a declaration of innocence (e.g., Ps 7:8), to deny there is any contradiction: the psalmist is only comparing himself with his enemies, and maintaining "not without cause, that, in respect of them, he was righteous" (*Com. Ps.* 7:8).[5] But if he finds no reference to guilt or innocence he is not likely to raise the subject at all. As a result, he passes without comment over the majority of the prayer psalms, never explaining why they make no issue of guilt or pardon at all.

But if he feels no need to justify his claim that the biblical saints "always have begun with appeasing" God and that we will readily see this "if we diligently ponder their prayers" (*Inst.* 3.20.9), he amply illustrates what he has in mind by the phrase "diligently ponder." Following what are no doubt well-established paths, he often finds a "plea for the forgiveness of sins" implied where none is stated. Any reference to God's anger "imports a tacit confession of sin," even in such phrases as "Cast not away thy servant in thy wrath" (*Com. Ps.* 27:9) or "Why hast thou cast us off forever? Why doth thy anger smoke against the flock of thy pastures?" (*Com. Ps.*

5. He had given the same, doubtless traditional, answer in *Inst.* 3.20.10 in a passage written for the 1539 edition. The psalmists are "comparing themselves with their enemies," so "it is no wonder if in this comparison they put forward their own righteousness and simplicity of heart in order that, from the equity of the cause itself, they might the more move the Lord to provide them with assistance."

74:1; see also *Com. Ps.* 79:5, 102:10). In any reference to sackcloth "we may perceive that in their mourning they were exercised to repentance," even in such phrases as "thou hast loosed my sackcloth" (*Com. Ps.* 30:11) or "when they were sick, my clothing was sackcloth" (*Com. Ps.* 35:13).

Even phrases such as "Thou hast made us to turn back from the enemy" are taken to be acknowledgements "that the fear by which they are now actuated was inflicted upon them as a punishment by God" (*Com. Ps.* 44:10). In one case, finding no sign of penitence at all, he argues (on the basis of the title and the phrase "I have cried to the Lord" in v. 4) that a separate penitential prayer must have preceded the present psalm; on this assumption he can say, "having acknowledged his sin before, he now takes into consideration only the merits of the present cause" (*Com. Ps.* 3:3).

A penitential reading of this sort seriously misconstrues the piety of the prayer psalms. Of the fifty or so examples of this genre represented in the Psalter, few even mention the psalmist's sin or guilt or plead for forgiveness, and there is only one (Psalm 51) in which this could be said to be the dominant theme.[6]

Praying to Motivate God

While he finds it to be no problem that "the saints do not always beg forgiveness of sins in so many words" (*Inst.* 3.20.9), there are aspects of the Psalms that do exercise him, and these will occupy us somewhat longer. The passages that elicit the most interesting and complex responses are those that suggest something "we must not imagine" of God, namely "that he acts contrary to his real character, or that he has changed his purpose" (*Com. Ps.* 25:6). They suggest this by seeking in many different ways to move God to act or, occasionally, to withdraw.

Calvin understands all talk of moving God to be language of accommodation, and on this understanding he employs it himself.

---

6. The count includes *Klagelieder* and two closely associated genres, *Danklieder* ("thank songs") and *Vertrauenspsalmen* ("psalms of confidence"). Apart from Psalm 51, pleas for forgiveness are joined with appeals of other kinds.

When he does so, he often introduces a parenthetical remark to alert the reader: "The reason why God seems to take no notice of our afflictions is, because he would have us to awaken him by means of our prayers; for when he hears our requests, (as if he began but then to be mindful of us,) he stretches forth his powerful hand to help us" (*Com. Ps.* 9:18). But he does not always do this. "The Holy Spirit, in dictating to the faithful this form of prayer, meant to testify that God is moved by such revilings to succor his people"; indeed, "the more insolent our enemies are against us, the more is God incited to gird himself to aid us" (*Com. Ps.* 102:8); "he is moved by the sight of our miseries to be merciful to us" (*Com. Ps.* 102:25).

It is easier to find passages like these, where Calvin speaks of God being moved by our troubles, than it is to find ones where he speaks of God being moved by our prayers. He appears to do so once in *Institutes* 3.20 (the chapter on prayer), when he writes, "they put forward their own righteousness and simplicity of heart in order that, from the equity of the cause itself, they might the more move the Lord to provide them with assistance"(*Inst.* 3.20.10). But he uses variations on this language throughout the commentary also to describe what the psalmists are seeking to do, without implying that they actually effect it.

His reticence is understandable. In truth God cannot be motivated to change, for God is immutable and impassible. This is fundamental to his theological stance and his piety. If it were not so, prayer itself would be impossible, as he argues in the chapter on prayer. "If [God] were not forever like himself, from his benefits a sufficiently firm reckoning could not be adduced to trust him and call upon him" (*Inst.* 3.20.26). In spite of his great sympathy for the psalmists, he is bound to see in all such attempts both a resistance to God's will, because they seek to move God, and a wavering faith, because they suppose God needs to be moved. They are therefore in conflict with his first and fourth rules for right prayer, to "submit completely to God's will" and to pray in the "sure hope that our prayer will be answered."

Under the circumstances, we might have expected him to draw as little attention to this feature as possible, a strategy not uncommon among pious commentators.[7] Instead he very often points the reader to it and explains what the psalmists are hoping to achieve by it. He describes them as adducing arguments, putting forth reasons, motives, and circumstances, complaining and expostulating, and employing other means as well.[8] Their purpose, put most simply, is to obtain or elicit something from God.[9] More often he uses verbs that indicate how they expect to affect God: to win God over, rouse, change, influence, induce, incline, move, or hasten God.[10] And he frequently adds adverbs, to indicate they expect by these means to move God the more, the more readily, the more easily, the more quickly.[11]

Furthermore, he takes a quite remarkable interest in the various means the psalmists employ. Of some psalms he is content to say, as he does of Psalm 55, that they urge "every consideration which could be supposed" (*Com. Ps.* 55 preface). But by the end of the commentary he has identified a large number of different means and devices, having given more attention to the psalmists' rhetoric of persuasion than most modern commentators. This is not the place to present a full account, so I shall be content with a summary overview.

One large set comprises the complaints against the psalmists' opponents, their malice and cruelty, their derision, that they act without cause, threaten extermination, and take encouragement from the psalmists' weakness, and the like. He recognizes that these

---

7. Among recent commentators Weiser (1962) is an example, although few modern commentaries have much to say about this.

8. The terms Calvin employs are *argumentum, ratio, causa, circumstantia, querimonia* and *expostulatio*

9. The verbs Calvin employs in this connection are *impetrare* (cf. Pss 5 intro.; 5:11; 38:5; 40:16; 80 intro.; 83 intro.; 86:1); *invenire* (cf. Ps 38:19); *elicere* (cf. Ps 40:11).

10. The verbs Calvin employs are *conciliare* (cf. Pss 5:4; 7:3; 9:1; 17:9; 27:7; 44:22; 59:4; 64:1; 69:20; 71:10; 74:1, 21; 79:9; 80:17; 86:2, 16; 89:51; 102:8; 140:1); *provocare* (cf. Pss 5:9; 22:6, 11; 38:11; 40:9; 41:5; 44:1; 79:4; 83:4; 89:5); *flectere* (cf. Pss 25:2; 27:9; 31:9; 38 intro; 38:6; 74:20; 89:47); *inducere* (cf. Pss 9:19; 27:9; 31:3); *inclinare* (cf. Pss 38:13; 57:4; 64 intro; 102:14); *movere* (cf. Pss 55 intro; 102:8); *permovere* (cf. Ps 39:5; *Inst.* 3.20.10); *accelerare* (cf. Ps 142:5).

11. The adverbs Calvin employs are *magis, plus, propensior, facilius, citius.*

31

are not simply cries of hurt. They have a rhetorical thrust: the point is "to render them more hateful [or more odious] in the sight of God" (*Com. Ps.* 35:26 [and 5:9]). And he notices that the psalmists heighten the effect by making use of rhetorical devices such as repetition (*Com. Ps.* 5:9), metaphor (*Com. Ps.* 7:2) and question (*Com. Ps.* 10:13).

Another set comprises what could be termed self-referential complaints, e.g., the greatness of the psalmists' misery, grief and distress, their poverty and need, that they are forsaken and have no one to help. These are not simply cries of hurt; the psalmists have a motive for dwelling upon such matters: they enhance the likelihood of a favorable hearing.

If one begins to read the psalms with an eye for their persuasive thrust, passages of this sort stand out immediately. Calvin goes on to identify many other types that are less often acknowledged. Among them are self-referential appeals that are not complaints but the opposite, something more like boasts. It is "for no other reason but to induce God to continue his goodness towards him" that David calls God's attention to his own previous thankfulness (*Com. Ps.* 40:9). "As a plea to induce God the more readily to have pity upon him" he proffers his own patience (as well as his humility and dejection; *Com. Ps.* 38:13, also v. 6). In another psalm he adduces two other reasons: "his own gentleness towards his neighbors, and the trust which he reposed in God" (*Com. Ps.* 86:2). In Psalm 143 "as elsewhere" his plea is "for in thee have I hoped," "this being something by which, in a sense, we lay God under obligation to us" (*Com. Ps.* 143:8). In short, Calvin includes among the psalmists' persuasive rhetorical devices even their assertions of thankfulness, patience, trust and hope.

An argument of another sort David "often adduces" is that others will benefit from his deliverance and be glad for it (*Com. Ps.* 40:16, cf. 5:11; 69:32). David phrases the same argument as a negative petition: "let not them that wait for thee be ashamed in me" (*Com. Ps.* 69:6). He protests his innocence "to induce God to show him favor," and "to give his protestation greater weight, he uses a [self-]imprecation" (*Com. Ps.* 7:3). And he calls to mind God's former favors and contrasts them with the present (*Com. Ps.* 27:9), a line of argument employed elsewhere (*Com. Ps.* 44:1; 74:2; 80:8, 17; 83:9).

"As a plea for obtaining greater favor" David puts forward "the long line of his ancestors, and the continual course of God's grace" (*Com. Ps.* 86:16). And "although God stands in no need of our praises" (*Com. Ps.* 40:9), David opens one psalm with praise in order to conciliate God (*Com. Ps.* 9:1), in another calls attention to praises he had previously offered "in order to elicit new favors" (*Com. Ps.* 40:11), and in yet another, "to obtain a longer life," he "draws an argument from praise," namely, that this is the purpose for which we are born and nourished (*Com. Ps.* 30:9).

Indeed the very vehemence of the psalmists' cries is meant to motivate God (*Com. Ps.* 27:7). "O God of our salvation!" is one of many forms of address they employ "to induce God to show them favor" (*Com. Ps.* 79:9). "The object in view" in presenting God's liberality before him "is that he should not leave unfinished the work of his hands" (*Com. Ps.* 80). They appeal to the brevity of human life "in order to excite God so much the more to pity" (*Com. Ps.* 39:5). "The more effectually to induce God to listen to his prayer," one psalmist calls upon all the godly to join in the request for Zion's welfare (*Com. Ps.* 102:14).

I find the range and detail of these observations quite remarkable, and I have given only a sample. Whether we accept them all or not, it must be granted that Calvin is attentive to an aspect of the prayer psalms that too often receives only cursory treatment. He is of course writing for an audience that shares his interest. Rhetoric had a central place in the sixteenth-century world of letters, as historians of the period have emphasized.[12] It is nevertheless striking that he employs this kind of analysis so extensively, given his unyielding conviction that it is neither necessary nor possible to persuade God at all.

12. Cf. Suzanne Selinger's comment, ". . . in the sixteenth century, rhetoric existed in a context that makes it intriguing as well as interesting to a historian. It existed in a world as conscious and self-conscious about language as, I think, only the last decade of the twentieth century has been, it was a world of discourse about the significance of discourse, one in which attention to discourse was a conceptual lingua franca" (1984: 154). See also her comments on "the fundamental significance of rhetoric in Renaissance humanism" (1984: 5–6).

As he comments on these passages he does feel obliged, to be sure, to pause now and then to remind the reader of this. In response to the question "Why do the wicked despise God?" he remarks, "It is, indeed, superfluous to bring arguments before God, for the purpose of persuading him to grant us what we ask" (*Com. Ps.* 10:13). He assures us that "God, indeed, does not need to receive information and incitement from us" (*Com. Ps.* 17:9), in response to the psalmist's complaint about "the ungodly, who go about to destroy me." And in reference to Ps 54:3, "for strangers are risen up against me, and the terrible ones have sought after my soul," he says sharply, "There was no necessity for his informing God of a fact which was already known to him" (*Com. Ps.* 54:2).

When David, "to move God to succor him . . . magnifies the greatness of his misery and grief by the number of his complaints," Calvin again reminds the reader that it is "not that God needs arguments to persuade him" (*Com. Ps.* 31:9). When David invokes the argument that others will benefit, he cautions, "not that it is necessary to allege reasons to persuade God" (*Com. Ps.* 40:16), and when David lays before God the danger that the faithful would otherwise be "exceedingly discouraged," he adds, "not that God has ever need of being put in mind of anything" (*Com. Ps.* 69:6).

Have the psalmists forgotten these self-evident truths? If they have, it is only for the moment; they know better. When the psalmist cries "Forsake me not, O Lord my God, and be not far from me," Calvin assures us that "David was, indeed, persuaded that God is always near to his servants, and that he delays not a single moment longer than is necessary" (*Com. Ps.* 38:21). Of another cry, "Awake to hasten for my help, and behold," he says, "Though David may use language of this description, suited to the infirmity of sense, we must not suppose him to have doubted before this time that his afflictions, his innocence, and his wrongs, were known to God" (*Com. Ps.* 59:4).

We may well ask how he knows this, but there is no doubt he thinks it important to offer this assurance to the reader. The assurance is often coupled with lines of argument I have mentioned before: the psalmists are distraught and acting under the pressure of the moment, the extreme trials they are experiencing are extenuating circumstances, and there are passages in which they admit their error and correct themselves.

It can hardly surprise us that this is the stance he takes. The sum of it is that prayers that take the form of God-persuading speech do not reflect the psalmists' strengths but their weaknesses, which we share. Far from admiring the psalmists for their boldness in seeking to motivate God, we ought to pity them that they are in this regard so much like ourselves.

If we are to admire them at all, it is because they hold nothing back. "They are not ashamed to confess their infirmity, nor is it proper to conceal the doubts which arise in their minds" (*Com. Ps.* 38:21). It is not proper because, as "we pour out our hearts before him," we must hold nothing back. Full self-disclosure in prayer is at the same time God's gracious invitation and an obligation God lays upon us; anything short of it is hypocrisy.

It is not, however, an end in itself, and there is only one right outcome: to keep our feelings under control and to submit to the divine will. "If we are anxiously desirous of obtaining his assistance, we must subdue our passion, restrain our impatience, and keep our sorrows within due bounds, waiting until our afflictions call forth the exercise of his compassion, and excite him to manifest his grace in succoring us" (*Com. Ps.* 10:18).

The legitimate role of speech to persuade God exists within the bounds of the subtle and complex dynamics of prayer in an introspective mode. Our prayers may work a change in us while we are mistakenly seeking to effect a change in God. Having said that God still permits us to make use of arguments, even though they are superfluous, Calvin adds, "It should always be observed, that the use of praying is, that God may be the witness of all our affections; not that they would otherwise be hidden from him, but when we pour out our hearts before him, our cares are hereby greatly lightened, and our confidence of obtaining our requests increases" (*Com. Ps.* 10:13).

God-persuading speech is of course full of anthropomorphic imagery, and he cautions his readers about it. Speaking of the line "Why standest thou afar off, O Jehovah?" he remarks, "It is in an improper sense, and by anthropathy, that the Psalmist speaks of

God as standing far off" (*Com. Ps.* 10:1). "Nothing can be hid from his eyes; but as God permits us to speak to him as we do to one another, these forms of expression do not contain any thing absurd, provided we understand them as applied to God, not in a strict sense, but only figuratively, according to the judgment which mere sense forms from the present appearance of things" (*Com. Ps.* 10:1). Does he mean to say that the psalmists themselves understood they were speaking "not in a strict sense, but only figuratively"? This is not entirely clear, although the passage I will cite next suggests this is what he has in mind. What is clear is that they employ this language to express thoughts that represent human infirmity rather than faith, "the judgment which mere sense forms from the present appearance of things." Here at least one might have supposed a charge of impropriety would stick, but Calvin evidently does not think so. He writes, "Whenever the faithful put the question, 'How long wilt thou forget me, O Lord?' 'Awake, why sleepest thou, O Lord?' (Ps. xiii.1; xliv.23; lxxix.5), they assuredly are not to be understood as attributing forgetfulness or sleep to him: they only lay before him the temptations which flesh and blood suggest to them in order to induce him speedily to succor them under the infirmity with which they are distressed" (*Com. Ps.* 89:39).

This puts a remarkably subtle spin on the psalmists' questions. They are not the assertive rhetorical challenges they appear to be; instead they represent what the psalmists are tempted to think when they yield to the suggestions of "flesh and blood." They voice them only to "lay before him the temptations" that troubled them so sorely. It is still the case that they do this to induce God to act speedily; the questions do not cease to be God-persuading speech. But a question laid before God as a "temptation" is quite different from a question put to God directly and rhetorically.

At this point Calvin sees what he expects to see, what he wishes to see. The psalmists' straightforward questions have been so overlaid with supposition they are no longer recognizable. Persuasive speech in the psalms has lost its bite, and taken on a markedly indirect, submissive, and introspective character; it has become part of the "unburdening" process that Calvin regards as one of the chief functions of prayer. Of Ps 38:21, for example, he says, "it is not at

Unfolding the Inmost Feelings of David

all wonderful that the saints, when they unburden themselves of their cares and sorrows into the bosom of God, should make their requests in language according to the feeling of the flesh" (*Com. Ps.* 38:21).

Praying to Motivate Oneself

The declaration "My shield is in God, who saves the upright in heart" (Ps 7:10) is not phrased as direct address to God. It is possible, therefore, to read it as an aside in which the psalmist addresses himself. Calvin has declarations of this sort in mind when he writes in the chapter on prayer, "Indeed, we may note this in the Psalms: that if the thread of prayer were broken, transition is sometimes made to God's power, sometimes to his goodness, sometimes to the faithfulness of his promises" (*Inst.* 3.20.13). He feels these sometimes abrupt transitions interrupt the flow of prayer, but believes they are necessary for our sakes. "It might seem that David, by inserting these statements inopportunely, mutilates his prayers, but believers know by use and experience that ardor burns low unless they supply new fuel" (*Inst.* 3.20.13).

Ps 7:10 and other passages like it are not necessarily self-address just because they are not formally addressed to God; they may be spoken aloud (and in prayer) for God's benefit rather than the psalmist's. Instead of supposing that they spring from a feeling "that ardor burns low," we could, for example, read them as forthright and self-assured declarations of confidence, advanced precisely as a claim upon God's reputation and patronage. That would astound Calvin, for he expects prayer to be a faith-struggle with the carnal and depraved self; it is only with great difficulty that believers rise to ardor and confidence.

As he reads the passage, therefore, Calvin does not question that the psalmist is speaking the words self-reflectively, and intends them to be self-assuring. He tells his readers to expect this frequently in the psalms. "It is not wonderful," he writes, "that David often mingles meditations with his prayers, thereby to inspire himself with true confidence." And he spells out what David is doing here:

"David, therefore, in order to continue in prayer with the same ardor of devotion and affection with which he commenced, brings to his recollection some of the most common truths of religion, and by this means fosters and invigorates his faith" (*Com. Ps.* 7:10). He finds these meditations in an extraordinary variety of passages, many of them in fact addressed directly to God and so quite different in form from a passage like Ps 7:10. The question put in Ps 10:1, "Why standest thou afar off, O Jehovah? and winkest at seasonable times in trouble?" is a particularly helpful example because it is so like passages that he identifies as God-motivating speech. He first assures us that David is speaking "through the infirmity of sense"; God is never "afar off." But his next point comes as something of a surprise: David "speaks thus not so much in the way of complaining, as to encourage himself in the confidence of obtaining what he desired" (*Com. Ps.* 10:1).

How can such a question raise the level of the psalmist's confidence? The process he has in mind is not well described in his exposition of Ps 10:1, but he elaborates it in many other passages. The assumption is that they are putting the questions to themselves, not to God, and providing their own answers. By dividing a verse rather awkwardly into a question and an answer, thus translating "O Lord! [Q:] where are thy former mercies? [A:] thou hast sworn to David in thy truth," he is able to find one passage where they occur together. Here "the prophet encourages himself, by calling to remembrance God's former benefits, as if his reasoning were that God can never be unlike himself, and that therefore the goodness which he manifested in old time to the fathers cannot come to an end" (*Com. Ps.* 89:49).

For the most part, however, Calvin must deal with passages in which only the questions appear. The answers he must supply himself, on the psalmists' behalf, and he does not hesitate to do so. When the question is put, "Shall the throne of iniquities have fellowship with thee, framing molestation for law?" he spells out the psalmist's reasoning for us: he "again derives an argument for confidence from the nature of God, it being impossible that he should show favor to the wicked, or sanction their evil devices" (*Com. Ps.* 94:20). He finds the same line of reasoning behind the question "Why do the wicked despise God? He saith in his heart, Thou wilt not require it"; as he explains, "Thus David, in the present passage, by setting before himself how unreasonable and intolerable it would be for the wicked to be allowed to despise God according to their pleasure, thinking he will never bring them to account, was led to cherish the hope of deliverance from his calamities" (*Com. Ps.* 10:13).

I have already mentioned a psalm passage that Calvin reads as God-persuading speech and self-persuading speech at the same time. The last citation is another example. The question "Why do the wicked despise God? He saith in his heart, Thou wilt not require it" is also identified as an argument to motivate God; in fact it elicits the comment that God "permits us to make use of them," as we have noted. Many other passages serve double-duty, so to speak, in this same way, among them the extended complaints about "my enemies" in Pss 41:5–9 and 71:10–11 (*Com. Ps.* 41:5; 71:10); the self-complaint "But I am a worm, and not a man" (*Com. Ps.* 22:6); the petitions to be kept "from the face of the ungodly" (*Com. Ps.* 17:9) and to "remember thy congregation which thou hast possessed of old" (*Com. Ps.* 74:2); the titles "God of vengeance" and "Judge of the earth" (*Com. Ps.* 94:1); and the declarations "I will tell of thy marvelous works" (*Com. Ps.* 9:1), "For thou art not a God that hath pleasure in wickedness (*Com. Ps.* 5:4), "thou hast been my strength" (*Com. Ps.* 27:9), and "For thy name's sake thou wilt lead and guide me" (*Com. Ps.* 31:3).

It is easy enough to see how these categories overlap in his mind. He understands both to be implicit arguments, and any motive or argument that could be supposed to move God must surely suffice to assure the psalmist also. Commenting on the phrase "thou hast been my strength," he remarks, "by recalling to mind God's former favors, he encourages himself to hope for more, and by this argument he moves God to continue his help, and not to leave his work imperfect" (*Com. Ps.* 27:9). He writes similarly of the phrase "remember thy congregation": "These benefits which they had received from God they set before themselves as an encouragement to their trusting in him, and they recount them before Him, the benefactor who bestowed them, as an argument with him not to forsake the work of his own hands" (*Com. Ps.* 74:2).

Praying for Vengeance

I turn now to the passages that Calvin does not mention at all in his chapter on prayer in the *Institutes*, the petitions for the death and destruction of the enemy, e.g., "Let death seize upon them, let them descend alive into the grave: for wickedness is in their dwelling, and in the midst of them" (*Com. Ps.* 55:15). In this case there is a hint that he would prefer to say as little as possible. Relatively early in the commentary he writes, "Here again occurs the difficult question about praying for vengeance, which, however, I shall dispatch in few words, as I have discussed it elsewhere" (*Com. Ps.* 28:4).[13] But he keeps coming back to it, and he involves himself in an extended exposition whenever such a petition appears.

"David's example . . . must not be alleged by those who are driven by their own intemperate passion to seek vengeance" (*Com. Ps.* 28:4). This is the point he makes repeatedly, and it seems to be the central focus of his concern. "We have already frequently spoken of the feelings with which David uttered these imprecations, and it is necessary here again to refresh our memories on the subject, lest any man, when giving loose reins to his passions, should allege the example of David in palliation or excuse" (*Com. Ps.* 40:14). He "affords no precedent to such as resent private injuries by vending curses on those who have inflicted them" (*Com. Ps.* 59:5). He emphasizes this because he regards it as "unquestionable, that if the flesh move us to seek revenge, the desire is wicked in the sight of God. He not only forbids us to imprecate evil upon our enemies in revenge for private injuries, but it cannot be otherwise than that all those desires which spring from hatred must be disordered" (*Com. Ps.* 28:4).

The effect of this is to make the decisive issue once again how well mind and will succeed in subduing involuntary thoughts and

---

13. Cf. Suzanne Selinger's comment, "in the sixteenth century, rhetoric existed in a context that makes it intriguing as well as interesting to a historian. It existed in a world as conscious and self-conscious about language as, I think, only the last decade of the twentieth century has been; it was a world of discourse about the significance of discourse, one in which attention to discourse was a conceptual lingua franca" (1984: 154). See also her comments on "the fundamental significance of rhetoric in Renaissance humanism" (1984: 5–6).

feelings. Prayers for vengeance are licit only if motives and feelings are entirely pure: "Before a man can, therefore, denounce vengeance against the wicked, he must first shake himself free from all improper feelings in his own mind. In the second place, prudence must be exercised, that the heinousness of the evils which offend us drive us not to intemperate zeal, which happened even to Christ's disciples, when they desired that fire might be brought from heaven to consume those who refused to entertain their Master (Luke ix.54)" (*Com. Ps.* 28:4). The critical locus is the inner self, as it was in the case of self-motivating and God-motivating speech. What we would expect him to say next is that just as the psalmists are not exempt from human infirmity in any other respect, so they are not here. Their prayers for vengeance are a complex mixture of faith and doubt, holy zeal and personal revenge, partly founded in a proper and commendable trust in God's promise of justice, but partly motivated as well by the unruly passions to which all flesh is heir.

In fact he says no such thing. He tells us instead that "David, being free from every evil passion, and likewise endued with the spirit of discretion and judgment, pleads here not so much his own cause as the cause of God" (*Com. Ps.* 28:4), that he "pleads not simply his own cause, nor utters rashly the dictates of passion, nor with unadvised zeal desires the destruction of his enemies; but under the guidance of the Holy Spirit he entertains and expresses against the reprobate such desires as were characterized by great moderation, and which were far removed from the spirit of those who are impelled either by desire of revenge or hatred, or some other inordinate emotion of the flesh" (*Com. Ps.* 35:4).

"Being free from every evil passion," David may even pray, "raise me up, and I will recompense them." But in this case an additional "two things are to be taken into account: First, David was not as one of the common people, but a king appointed by God, and invested with authority; and, secondly, it is not from an impulse of the flesh, but in virtue of the nature of his office, that he is led to denounce against his enemies the punishment which they had merited" (*Com. Ps.* 41:10). Few are in that position, and it is not given to many to pray so rightly: "I acknowledge, indeed, that not a few, while they pretend a similar confidence and hope, nevertheless, recklessly rush beyond the bounds of temperance and moderation. But that which David beheld by the unclouded eye of faith, he also uttered with a zeal becoming a sound mind; for having devoted himself to the cultivation of piety, and being protected by the hand of God, he was aware that the day was approaching when his enemies would meet with merited punishment" (*Com. Ps.* 109:20).

For the most part, "Even those who are naturally inclined to gentleness and humanity, who desire to do good to all men, and wish to hurt nobody, whenever they are provoked, burst forth into a revengeful mood, carried away by a blind impetuosity" and "begin to howl with the wolves" (*Com. Ps.* 17:4). Therefore, "it becomes us to bear in mind what I have previously stated, that the man who would offer up such a prayer as this in a right manner, must be under the influence of zeal for the public welfare; so that, by the wrongs done to himself personally, he may not suffer his carnal affections to be excited . . ." (*Com. Ps.* 79:6).

The claims for David, however, are made without qualification, and seem even to heighten as the commentary progresses. Speaking of the petition I cited at the beginning of this section, he writes, "In imprecating this curse he was not influenced by *any* bad feeling towards them, and must be understood as speaking not in his own cause but in that of God, and under the immediate guidance of his Spirit" (*Com. Ps.* 55:5 [emphasis added]). He finds in Psalm 109 a "David, who, free of *all* inordinate passion, breathed forth his prayers under the influence of the Holy Spirit" (*Com. Ps.* 109:6 [emphasis added]); "in this instance God elevated his spirit above *all* earthly considerations, stript him of *all* malice, and delivered him from the influence of turbulent passions, so that he might, with holy calmness and spiritual wisdom, doom the reprobate and castaway to destruction" (*Com. Ps.* 109:19 [emphasis added]).

I find this an extraordinary departure from his usual approach to the psalms.[14] David has taken on the role of Christ the

14. Brevard Childs is generally approving of Calvin's handling of the imprecatory psalms, but remarks, "However, would it not have been more theologically consistent for him to have recognized also the elements of personal anger and frustration . . . rather than to have pictured David, the psalmist, as

Vindicator, and this not as a type of the divine King to come, but in his own historical office as king of Israel. It is no wonder he wants to safeguard this, "that no one may rashly take for an example what David here spoke by the special influence of the Holy Spirit" (*Com. Ps.* 109:19). But is it possible that others, also "appointed by God, and invested with authority," and acting "not from an impulse of the flesh, but in virtue of the nature of [their] office," may likewise be "led to denounce against [their] enemies the punishment which they had merited"? I should like to keep this question in mind when we turn in the third part of this study to the preface he wrote for the commentary in July 1557.

FROM THE COMMENTARY TO THE CHAPTER ON PRAYER

By the time Calvin had completed the manuscript for the commentary, if not before, he had worked out the stance toward the prayer psalms he would assume as he revised the chapter on prayer. The rules by which the psalms are explicitly judged in the chapter are already implicit in the commentary. The same lines of defense are mounted on the psalmists' behalf. The same assumption is made about their unfailingly penitential attitude. And the readers' attention is directed primarily to their inner life and internal struggles.

There are nevertheless differences, although they are primarily matters of emphasis. Coming to the commentary from the chapter on prayer, one is surprised by the attention given to the psalmists' persuasive rhetoric. If one read only the chapter on prayer one would never know how much this interested him. There he seems to emphasize his disapproval by the very terms he uses to describe it, preferring "expostulate with God" and the like to the relatively mild "(seek) to move God" (the latter appears only once in the chapter, *Inst.* 3.20.10).

Proceeding the other way, from the commentary to the chapter on prayer, one is surprised by the sharpness of his criticism. If one read only the commentary one would not feel the full force of

---

an Old Testament saint with zeal only for God's kingdom?" (1989: 263).

his unease.[15] On the whole he handles the psalmists more gently and graciously there, explaining their failures and excesses rather than rebuking them, at times extending the argument to shield them from criticism. In the chapter on prayer the disquiet lies nearer the surface; although he still does not allow that they did so willfully, he makes it clear they often went too far and stood in need of forgiveness.

The two works are quite different in genre, and this no doubt accounts for much of the difference in emphasis. But it may also be the case that after 1557 some of his earlier misgivings had begun to reassert themselves; it was never as easy for him to approve David as he wished it to be.

15. Compare, for example, his comments on Ps 39:13 in *Inst.* 3.20.16 with those in the commentary.

4

Appropriating Psalter Piety

As I have already suggested, Calvin's appropriation of the piety of David and the psalms is no less revealing than his exposition of it. The form this appropriation takes is set out with unusual clarity in the letter he wrote in July 1557 as a preface to his commentary on the book of Psalms.

THE LETTER TO HIS READERS

It is particularly this preface, "John Calvin to the godly readers sends greeting," which shows how personally he had come to be involved with the psalms. It contains one of the few autobiographical passages in all his theological writings, and it turns out to be an interweaving of his life story with the psalms and experiences of David. He has come to feel that his own life experience has made him a particularly sensitive interpreter. "The readers too will find, if I mistake not, that when I unfold the inmost feelings of David and others, I discourse on them no otherwise than as on things well known to me." His own struggles and conflicts have been "no small help to me in understanding the Psalms, with the result that I did not journey as it were in an unknown region" (Calvin 1965: 23).

We therefore need no special warrant for relating Calvin's response to the Psalter to his own life experience. He has given thought to the connection himself, and even called his readers' attention to it. If I now supplement what he himself reports, it is to note that he is writing the preface itself at a particularly interesting moment in his life—a time when, at the age of forty-eight and after years of struggle, conflict and uncertainty, his position and that of his partisans in Geneva seemed at last to be secure.

Several events had combined to bring this about. Four years earlier a convicted Spanish heretic had entered Geneva in disguise and had been arrested, tried, and burned at the stake. The affair had been painful for Calvin, who had wanted him beheaded instead, but it had turned the elections decidedly in his favor. A year and a half after this, a fairly harmless civil disturbance had been used as a pretext by Calvin's supporters to drive members of the opposition out of the city; one did not escape in time, and was beheaded. Meanwhile, a flood of French Protestant refugees had been pouring into Geneva, severely taxing its space and resources, but adding substantially to the number of Calvin's supporters. The Calvin party moved quickly to consolidate its position by obtaining admission to citizenship for a larger and larger number of these refugees, thereby providing itself with a secure majority.

By the time Calvin gave his lectures on the book of Psalms he was assured that his supporters would win the general elections and be in the majority in the city councils. His long controversy with the magistrates over the church's right to excommunicate had finally been resolved in his favor. While persons in such a position are likely to find a certain satisfaction in what they have achieved, they are also likely to find themselves reflecting on the checkered path that led to it, gathering the disparate moments of their past into the kind of self-portrait they can both believe and accept, and perhaps even trust to the world.

As Calvin pictures himself in the preface he falls far short of David's virtues. At the same time he sees himself very much like David, given to outbursts and often overwhelmed by strong emotions. And also like David he has been harassed and frustrated by enemies, who suffered at his hands only because they were impossibly stubborn and intractable. The tone is hardly conciliatory; the pain of their enmity still rankles. But he finds in David a model and a comfort, his own nearest counterpart in the Bible.

Two Modes of Appropriation

When we turn to the preface to see what effective use he makes of the psalms, we find him developing not one but two trajectories, relating the psalms to himself and his own experience in two quite different ways. The first cannot be missed, for he refers to it explicitly, describes it in detail, and urges his readers to share it. The second is more easily overlooked, for he simply models it and applies it to himself.

One trajectory certainly reflects the way he sees himself as a person, that is, as one who shares all the common human frailties. The other seems to reflect his perception of himself as a public figure, divinely appointed to a task he had not sought and would never have chosen. They are strikingly different in tone, but to a remarkable degree both center in the affective aspect of life and how it must be managed, an indication once again that this is one of the central issues the psalms raise for him.

As a Mirror of the Soul

When Calvin says he is "wont to call this book, not without cause, 'The Anatomy of all the parts of the soul,'" he is speaking of the use that is accessible to everyone, "for not an affection will a man find in himself, an image of which is not reflected in this glass" (Calvin 1965: 16). The passage is often cited, the image portrayed in charming and delightful colors. What Calvin has in mind is considerably more somber, for he continues,

> Nay, all the griefs, sorrows, fears, misgivings, hopes, cares, anxieties, in short, all the troublesome emotions with which the minds of men are wont to be agitated, the Holy Spirit has here pictured to the life. The other scriptures contain the commands which God enjoined His servants to bear to us. But here are prophets themselves talking with God,

because they lay bare all their inmost thoughts, invite or hale every one of us to examine himself in particular, lest aught of the many infirmities to which we are liable, or of the many vices with which we are beset should remain hidden. (Calvin 1965: 16)

To be sure, the picture he gives of the book of Psalms is not wholly negative; he finds "faith, patience, fervor, zeal and uprightness" represented there as well (Calvin 1965: 18). But as this passage shows, and as we have come now to expect, what makes the Psalter such a "rare and surpassing benefit" for us is its capacity to reflect back to us the thoughts and feelings that vex and trouble us, and even beset us as infirmities and vices. By showing us our inner selves and helping us to recognize what is there, the psalms invite us to self-examination and cleanse us "from hypocrisy, that most noisome pest." Even though it sometimes happens that the psalmists' faith is "not so active as were to be wished" (Calvin 1965: 17), they at least "lay bare all their inmost thoughts" when they talk to God (Calvin 1965: 16). Whatever their failings, they speak with astonishing honesty and candor, and do not hide their inmost feelings as (he implies) he and his readers are likely to do.

This essentially purgative use of the psalms provides a counterbalance to Calvin's first rule of right prayer, which would seem to forbid any such outpouring of troublesome thoughts and feelings out of regard for God's holiness and awesome majesty.[1] Pent-up emotions and vexatious thoughts can find an outlet in prayer, and the psalms provide both a warrant and a vehicle for their release. They show us that we are not alone; the prophets and saints were troubled as we are. If even David was caught up in turbulent emotions, we must not be surprised to find that we are also. But above all, as the metaphor of the mirror suggests, the psalms help us to see and recognize ourselves. They stand apart from us, and so they provide the distancing that self-recognition requires.

---

1. That the first rule does not forbid this he makes clear as he sets out the rule: "Now I do not here require the mind to be so detached as never to be pricked or gnawed by vexations, since, on the contrary, great anxiety should kindle in us the desire to pray" (*Inst.* 3.20.4).

Self-awareness is not an end in itself, however, nor is it enough to be sincere and open about whatever it is we think and feel, even if this may sometimes be as far as the psalms can take us. Sincerity of this sort rises above hypocrisy, but it still falls well short of what is pleasing and acceptable to God. It would be loathsome to be satisfied with ourselves as we are. Self-recognition should show us how much we need God's grace, prompt us to self-examination and repentance, move us to hearken to "the other scriptures" that bear to us the commands of God, and make us receptive to the teachings of the Spirit, sent by God "to tell us what is right and temper our emotions."

As a Model and Warrant for Dealing with the Enemy

A quite different use appears when Calvin's self-identification with David leads him to associate his own enemies with David's, and his response to them with the cries against the enemy in the Psalms. Here he thinks of himself as agitated by troublesome people rather than troublesome thoughts and feelings, and as striving against external enemies rather than internal infirmities and vices. The ethos is no longer one of self-examination and humble repentance but of complaint, conflict and combat. Readers who benefit by his commentary should be assured

> that by the ordinary experience of conflicts with which the Lord has exercised me, I have been in no ordinary degree assisted, not only in adapting to my immediate use whatever of doctrine I was permitted to draw from hence, but also in that it opened to me a more ready way towards understanding the purpose of each of the writers of the Psalms. And as David holds the chief place among them, it was no small help to me in obtaining a fuller understanding of the complaints he makes of the inward mischiefs of the church, that I had suffered the same things which he deplores, or similar to them, from enemies of the church who were of her own household. (Calvin 1965: 18)

Indeed he feels that David's experience is offered to him as a model: "so that I knew the more assuredly that whatsoever that most illustrious prince and prophet endured, was held out to me for an ensample" (Calvin 1965: 18).

As he proceeds his account begins to take on the sharp invective of the plaint psalms. He describes himself as "racked by the malignity of those who ceased not to assail myself and my ministry with venomous slanders" (Calvin 1965: 21). He speaks scathingly of those who opposed him. "For five whole years had I to fight without ceasing to preserve order, since froward men were furnished with overgrown influence, and some too of the common people, seduced by the enticements they held out to them, sought to obtain the power of doing what they pleased without control ... Many, too, through poverty and hunger, or insatiable ambition, or a vile lust of gain, became so mad, that by throwing everything into confusion, they would rather destroy themselves and us, than continue in a state of order" (Calvin 1965: 21). And he justifies the violent outcome: "Nor, to such a pass had they come, was there any other way of putting a stop to their wicked machinations, than in the shameful slaughter of them," though this was "indeed a mournful sight." He would rather they had listened to "wholesome counsels" (Calvin 1965: 21).

PUTTING THE TWO TOGETHER

This is the person who believes that even those racked with terrible pain ought to submit humbly and without complaining to what God has ordained. The disparity is sharpened by his well-known reluctance to share with others this prerogative for complaining, well illustrated by an incident in January 1546, when a certain Pierre Ameaux, a member of the highest of the city councils, complained to a private gathering in his home that Calvin was nothing but a wicked man, a Picard[2] who preached false doctrine. As François Wendel recounts the episode,

---

2. Calvin was born in Noyon, a cathedral town in Picardy (a province north of Paris), but the term "Picard" had insulting connotations of the sort regional designations often acquire.

The Magistrates offered to make the culprit beg Calvin's pardon on bended knees before the Council of the Two Hundred, but Calvin found this an insufficient reparation, and declared that he would not go up into a pulpit again until they had given him satisfaction. The case was then heard over again, and on April 8th Ameaux was sentenced to walk all round the town, dressed only in his shirt, bare-headed and carrying a lighted torch in his hand, and af-ter that to present himself before the tribunal and cry to God for mercy . . . A pastor of the countryside dared to criticize Calvin's attitude in this affair: he was immediately unfrocked. (Wendel 1963: 86)

Calvin was understandably sensitive to Ameaux's charge that he preached false doctrine, for it challenged the very basis of his authority in Geneva, which rested less on his formal status (he held no civic office) than on his reputation as a biblical scholar and theo-logian. Even so, his response seems spiteful, a vindictive demand for personal satisfaction.

Would he have conceded this himself? Two passages we have already cited from the commentary suggest he may have been ready to do so now, looking back on the incident after some eleven years. He finds it to be "unquestionable" that, "if the flesh move us to seek revenge, the desire is wicked in the sight of God," and God expressly forbids it (*Com. Ps.* 28:4). At the same time he knows that "even those who are naturally inclined to gentleness and humanity, who desire to do good to all men, and wish to hurt nobody, whenever they are provoked, burst forth into a revengeful mood, carried away by a blind impetuosity; especially when we see all right and equity overthrown, the confusion so blinds us, that we begin to howl with the wolves" (*Com. Ps.* 17:4).

The shift to "we" suggests he is speaking here of his own ex-perience, and the passage sounds almost like an apology for the way he had handled incidents just like this one. In fact many of his expositions on vengeance in the commentary have this almost-autobiographical and apologetic cast.

Whatever regret he may have come to feel about this affair, however, he does not appear to be at all inhibited by self-doubt when he denounces his opponents in the preface to the commentary. It is troubling to recall that in this one regard he finds no self-doubt in David either, or any reason for it, for there is no fault at all to be found in him. When David hurls invectives at his enemies and prays that they may be humiliated or worse, he is acting out of righteous indignation and holy zeal, not out of personal rancor or enmity. He is defending not himself but his office as prince and prophet, and it is necessary and proper that he should do so. His opponents have set themselves against God's sovereign will and the authority God has bestowed upon him, so they are not his personal enemies but the enemies of God.

If Calvin finds this distinction important for a proper understanding of David's motives, he may well think it relevant to his own. The preface itself suggests that he is in fact thinking along these lines. He wants it clearly understood that his present position in Geneva owes nothing to personal ambition; he is there only because others had prevailed upon him. Having first come to Geneva quite by accident he had not wanted to remain there, and after the city council had banished and forcibly expelled him he had not wished to return. This insistent separation of office and person, duty and personal preference, also gives him leave to threaten to withdraw his services if his demands are not met, just as he refused to preach until the magistrates agreed to take harsher action against Ameaux.

If this prerogative, and the particular appropriation of psalm piety that accompanies it, attaches to the office rather than the person, we can understand why he does not propose it for general use. The plaint psalms provide no general warrant for persons to complain about each other, and no license at all to complain about those whom God has set in authority over them. A special warrant is involved, which has its analog in the divine realm. Just as God may bring complaints against us, but we must learn not to complain against God even in our hearts, so Calvin may assail his opponents, but they may not speak against him even in their homes. The same principle applies to the determination of need. As God does not ask us what we need, knowing better than we do what is good for us, so kings, pastors and magistrates are required to care wisely for the poor, but they are not obliged to listen patiently to all their grievances.

The warrant is, however, balanced by an obligation that also has its analog in the divine realm, in this case Calvin's understanding of God's "wrath." Just as God, in punishing us, appears to us to be enraged, but there "is no such emotion in God," the anger existing solely in "the perception and feeling of the sinner who is punished," so those who by virtue of their divinely appointed office judge, censure and rebuke others must rise above all such passions as hurt, anger, and resentment.

In this respect the two rather different uses he makes of psalm piety may be viewed as complementary. The first provides a means for overcoming the vexing and involuntary thoughts and emotions that beset us. The second provides a model for the legitimate exercise of authority in times of conflict, a circumstance in which these personal feelings must be overcome. If they are not equally applicable to everyone, it is because not all persons are responsible to exercise authority.

In another respect, however, the two uses diverge rather than engage. One recognizes turbulent emotions in David and the other psalmists, which they and all believers must identify in themselves and continually strive to overcome. The other takes as its model prayers of David for which it is claimed that all such improper personal feelings have in fact been overcome.

Why does he go to such remarkable lengths to justify David's prayers for vengeance? As we have seen, he makes the extraordinary claim in his exposition of Psalm 109 that "God elevated his spirit above all earthly considerations, stript him of all malice, and delivered him from the influence of turbulent passion, so that he might, with holy calmness and spiritual wisdom, doom the reprobate and castaway to destruction" (*Com. Ps.* 109:19). Is this wholly because he sees in David a type of Christ, or is he hinting something of the same for himself and others who oppose the enemies of God and his Church?

Although he would certainly not claim for himself all that he claims for David, he may well consider the difference between himself and David to be one of degree rather than kind. He is, after all, somehow able to recognize in this divinely-enabled prince and prophet "free from every evil passion" the same David who is "affected by disquietude and trouble" and "not altogether exempted from human infirmity" (*Com. Ps.* 38:10). We are left with the impression that the thoughts and emotions that troubled David as a person did not intrude when he was empowered by the Spirit to act against the enemies of God and in defense of his office, and if we allow that his claims for himself would be far less categorical, it is at least possible to read the account he gives of himself in the preface in very much the same way.

Would the diagnostic use of the psalms as an "anatomy of the soul" at least serve as a counterbalance and restraint to this? I think it possible, but the "anatomy" can be employed in so many ways this is not a foregone conclusion. We could imagine it leading him to recognize the role personal feelings played even in his dealings with the "enemies of God," at least tempering the rather frightening self-confidence he brings to the task. But we could also imagine it having the opposite effect, leading him to feel that any self-doubts and anxieties he may have about these dealings were themselves the "vexing and troublesome emotions" he must struggle to overcome.

5

Recognizing the Piety
of the Prayer Psalms

THE BASIC HERMENEUTICAL MOVE that allowed Calvin to bring together so easily his theological conviction and his historical interest succeeded rather too well, for it effectively silenced the prayer
psalms as witnesses to their own intention. It is not that the psalms
offered no resistance; we have noted on more than one occasion
that he was obliged to reach rather far to make his exposition
appear reasonable.[1] To this point, however, I have not provided

1. As one would expect, when modern scholars find the Psalms resist-
ing their own sense of what psalm piety ought to be they do much the same.
Hans-Joachim Kraus (1986: 137), sharing Calvin's reluctance to accept that the
psalmists ever willfully reproached God, could only bring himself to say that
the "pressing questions, 'Why?,' 'How long?' . . . *often border on being* reproaches
and complaints against God" (emphasis added). Helmer Ringgren (1963: 27)
wrote that "The main concern in the Psalms is not the welfare of the psalmist,
but the glory of God'"—a position much like Calvin's—and justified it by the
following line of reasoning: "An important feature of the religion of the Psalms
is its theocentric or God-centered character. It is God and not man who is
the focus of the psalmist's interest. This does not mean that human concerns
are ignored, but they are, for the most part, subordinated to divine purposes.
The theocentric attitude is not at all points consistently affirmed. Sometimes
it must assert itself in competition with an anthropocentric or man-centered
attitude. But a strong theocentric tendency is nonetheless present, *even if at
times it can only be detected by reading between the lines*" (emphasis added).
It would be easy to multiply examples, but all too often the psalms' resistance

55

a summary overview of their own implicit self-understanding because I have wanted to present Calvin's view as clearly and faithfully as possible. I must now sketch this self-understanding at least briefly to illustrate how very different their piety is from Calvin's representation of it.

My account will differ considerably from what one would find in those works that have come to be regarded as more or less standard treatments of the subject; in my judgment they share too many of Calvin's preconceptions to be entirely reliable guides.[2] It will differ as well from the views of a number of scholars whose work has been moving in somewhat the same direction as my own.[3] I do not

---

is simply ignored: Kraus (1986: 127) simply asserts that "in the prayers of the national community" the "question of the 'why' of the historical catastrophe is answered in the assumption of the divine judgment" when in fact a penitential stance is not at all typical of these psalms.

2. A representative sampling can be found in the work of three prominent scholars: Artur Weiser (1962), Claus Westermann (1981; 1989) and Hans-Joachim Kraus (1986; 1988; 1989). While there are significant differences among them, the audiences they address are expected to identify readily with the essential dynamics of psalm piety, even it if they find biblical Israel's cultic practices and this-worldly orientation foreign to their own experience. Issues of piety are Weiser's central concern; in the course of his exposition the psalms are appropriated for and sometimes corrected by a Christian piety in the tradition of the reformers. Kraus, for all his frequent references to Luther and Calvin, has much less to say about psalmic prayer and the dynamics of psalm piety; he gives his attention primarily to other matters, although he clearly stands in the same tradition. When he comes to write of the meaning of the psalms for the Church, however, he often finds the plaint psalms addressing the Church's social conscience, as does Westermann. Indeed Westermann writes as an advocate of the biblical lament tradition on the ground that it gives suffering a legitimate voice, and he mourns its loss in the Church. Nevertheless his position is not as much a departure as some have made it out to be; within his larger scheme lament is structurally subordinated to praise. To effect this he follows a path taken also by Weiser and Kraus (and many others), invoking the surety of divine compassion, the notion that biblical Israelites valued praise of God above life itself, and the transformation within the psalmist that certain plaint-psalm motifs (the so-called "confession of trust," "certainty of a hearing," and "sudden change of mood") are said to exhibit. In one very important respect, however, all three differ from Calvin: none has given remotely comparable attention to the suasive rhetoric of the plaint psalms.

3. I refer in particular to Moshe Greenberg (1983); Walter Brueggemann

represent it, therefore, as the consensus of biblical scholarship at the present time—there is none—and I will not attempt here to provide detailed support from the biblical text. I am content to reserve that for a future study, building upon the groundwork I am now laying down. Before I begin, however, it may be useful to explain what I have in mind by the word piety when I am representing my own approach to the Psalter rather than Calvin's.

When I speak of a piety I refer to shared perceptions of, attitudes toward, and responses to the divine. I say shared, because it is piety as a social-religious phenomenon that I have in mind. In the Psalter we are dealing with a shared piety; the conventional language of the psalms assures us of that. I regard perceptions, attitudes and responses as focal concerns because they are essential to the dynamics of a living piety, and I link them together because they interact. This interaction is well represented in prayer, so we should be able to discern it in the Psalter.

Prayer is only one manifestation of a piety, to be sure, but it can be particularly revealing. When those who share a particular piety engage in prayer, they do so with a common understanding, often quite comprehensive, about what they may and indeed ought to say in prayer and what they must not say. They share a sense of how they may expect God to deal with them, and how they may in turn expect to deal with God. Implicit understandings of this sort are best discerned in the prayers themselves; they give us more

---

(1984; 1985); Patrick D. Miller (1986; 1993; 1994); Craig C. Broyles (1988); and Samuel E. Balentine, (1993). Of these the best account of biblical prayer as suasion is certainly Miller's 1993 article, although it omits to mention the vow, which is one of the most obvious means of suasion. Greenberg intentionally leaves the Psalms out of consideration on the ground that they are learned compositions that cannot be trusted to reflect lay piety. Balentine also focuses primarily on prayers outside the Psalter, but for other reasons: the Psalms provide no narrative context, and they have already been thoroughly studied by form critics. In my view, the Psalms and the prose prayers are remarkably similar in the essential dynamics of their implicit piety, whatever one may say about differences in their mode of composition, and there are still important questions to put to the Psalms that form criticism has not addressed. This is the stance taken by Miller (1994), where the working corpus includes the Psalms together with prayers in prose and prophetic material.

direct access to the functioning dynamics of a living piety than anything people may say about prayer to themselves or to others.[4]

Thus far I have spoken of Psalter piety in the singular for the simple reason that Calvin did not distinguish more than one. I shall continue to do so for simplicity's sake, although I do not wish to foreclose the possibility that several rather different pieties may be discerned in the book of Psalms. There is certainly more than one represented in the biblical corpus as a whole. What I think I can claim to be describing is the predominant piety to be found in the Psalter, the one represented by the majority, at least, of the plaint psalms, thank songs and hymns, which together make up the bulk of the book.

Recognizing the Dissonance

While Calvin, to his credit, recognized that the book of Psalms does not always follow his rules for framing prayer duly and properly, he found a way, as we have seen, to turn even those aspects that most distress him into a support for his own piety. In fact he accomplished this almost effortlessly. He simply took it for granted that the psalmists intended to follow the rules, but often failed to do so because they were so very like ourselves; and he did not doubt that they were as distressed by their failings as he would be and as anxious to overcome them by earnest striving.

It is this presumption that led him to value the psalms above all for their introspective capacity, the psalmists' willingness to "lay bare all their innermost thoughts" in prayer and the encouragement they give all believers to do the same. They may not always be models of proper prayer, but they are at least open, forthright, honest, candid and sincere.[5] Since this is the way they are often valued

---

4. The means of suasion are particularly helpful, as Greenberg (1983: 12–13) has noted. "The motivating sentence of a petitionary prayer is revealing for the pray-er's conception of God, since one is persuaded to do what is shown to be most consonant with one's attributes and interests."

5. This is, of course, not uniquely a Christian perspective. Greenberg (1983: 49), for example, elaborates upon the phrase "to pour out one's soul [*nepeš*] before God" much as Calvin might have done. It means "to expose

from the pulpit and lectern today, and a use to which they are often put in pastoral counseling, we are dealing here with one of the more lasting and important consequences of the approach to the Psalter that Calvin represents.

Quite apart from the fact that there is simply no way to judge such a thing from the wording of a psalm—imagine someone claiming to prove from their liturgies that Presbyterians are more sincere than Methodists or Baptists, or Christians than Jews!—the very notion is a distraction. If the psalms say and do things we would not put into prayer ourselves, we should not suppose it is because they have been more honest; it is rather that they have a different understanding of what one ought to say in prayer, in short, a different sense of piety.

In my judgment, we will not begin to understand the piety of the psalms until we recognize this. Their sense of what is appropriate in prayer has remarkably little in common with the one set forth in Calvin's rules. They revel in spirited engagement with God rather than devout resignation. Their complaints are typically very direct, even feisty.[6] They often speak as though God were part of the problem, as Psalm 39 does when it asks God to "look away"—Calvin's parade example of unlawful petition. When they do so, they can be indignant, reproachful and even bitingly ironic. On the other hand, they do not regard it as improper to be ingratiating and proffer inducements. They can represent themselves as helpless and piti-ful, or put forward a claim of unshakable confidence and trust, and often do both together. They know what it is to beg forgiveness, but they do not do so every time they find themselves in trouble. They present themselves to God more often as victims than as sinners. And when they cry to be delivered from their troubles and those

---

one's innermost being, revealing its secret concerns without reservation, without withholding anything—to speak all that is in one's mind with utter sincerity and candor." But once we have recognized that petitonary biblical prayer is suasive speech, as Greenberg himself has so aptly illustrated, how can we continue to ascribe to it such utterly ingenuous, defenseless and innocent self-abandon?

6. The prayer psalms observe a less formal protocol in addressing God than people in the books of Samuel observe in addressing David; for the latter see Kyu Nam Jung (1979).

who trouble them, they look for deliverance and nothing less; they do not pray for patience and fortitude to bear it, or concede the outcome in advance by deferring to God's sovereign will or superior judgment.

If we start where Calvin starts, this is bound to seem gratuitously and outrageously impertinent, irreverent, and impious. To the psalmists, however, Calvin's attitude (and that of much traditional Christian piety, I suspect) would surely seem unaccountably and irresponsibly obsequious, groveling, and servile. The difference, not surprisingly, is both religious and cultural. In biblical Israel the injured party is expected to complain and to present the grievance as persuasively as possible.[7] In the process there is even room for *chutzpah*, just as there is in biblical Israelite culture generally, so there is nothing remarkable that it should appear in the prayer psalms.[8] The psalmists could easily imagine God replying in kind, as the prophets, not to mention the divine speech "out of the whirlwind" in the book of Job (chaps. 38–41), plainly demonstrate.

If the psalmists speak this way, it is because it seems self-evident to them that psalmody works its effect upon God, not upon themselves, and everything about it—including its poetic form—is designed to enhance this and bring it about. In this way psalmody gives human beings a voice in those matters that most vitally affect their lives, either offering the encouraging praise and thanks that God delights in, or rousing God to action in a crisis by making the most effective plaints and appeals they can manage.[9] They do not feel they must submit humbly and penitently to whatever God ordains. There is always the possibility that God can be persuaded—or

7. In fact suasive speech is employed for inter-human petitions and requests generally. As E. S. Gerstenberger (1980: 17–63) and Greenberg (1983: 19–37) have shown, the forms used for inter-human petition provide the social analogy for petitionary prayer.

8. Cf. J. J. Petuchowski (1972: 4–5), "Prayer, if we think about it carefully, is actually a supreme manifestation of impertinence, of *chutzpah*. But such is the unique Jewish stance towards God that, according to one view in the Talmud, '*Chutzpah*, even against God, is of avail.'" The reference is to *b. Sanh.* 105a.

9. As J. J. M. Roberts (1975) has shown, the difference between biblical Israel and its neighbors in this regard has often been greatly exaggerated.

provoked, if it comes to that—to change course and act on their behalf. The future may still be open, the final decision not yet made.

Thus the psalmists petition, not to seek out a discrete and sympathetic heavenly confidant to whom they may pour out their troubles, hoping to find inner peace and consolation by submitting to a sovereign and unfailingly benevolent divine will, but to seek redress by mounting an appeal to heaven itself where the ultimate power to effect change resides.[10] The point of their prayers is not to express themselves to God, but to impress their situation upon God in the hope that God will take action to correct it. They do not suppose this will be easy, or the persuasive appeals they put forward would not be so elaborate or crafted with such care; moreover, they know from experience that God may not listen even to fervent and repeated pleas, for they frequently testify of this themselves.

ALLOWING FOR CULTURAL AND HISTORICAL DISTANCE

The piety of the prayer psalms as I have just described it differs from Calvin's representation in all the aspects I have enumerated above: in the responses to God it regards as appropriate, necessary and productive; in the attitudes toward God it holds to be acceptable, responsible, and justified; and in its very perception of God as one whose thoughts, feelings, motives, and actions correspond to a significant degree with what humans expect and experience in each other and themselves.

The remarkable thing is that Calvin saw much of this himself, as we have often noted above. He recognized that the psalms did in fact "expostulate" with God, challenge God's judgments, and make

---

10. Broyles (1988) has quite properly emphasized that complaint psalms function as appeals. His study of psalms that complain directly against God is an important contribution to our understanding of psalm piety. I think he is wrong, however, to accept the widely-held notion that the psalmists experienced a crisis of faith whenever they perceived God to be acting contrary to divine promises. The complaint psalms show well enough that they had developed a conventional way to deal with this situation, and if they had, they cannot have been taken unawares.

extensive use of rhetoric to persuade God to act favorably upon their appeals. He could not conceive, however, that the psalmists would do such things deliberately. Since he could not entertain that even as a possibility, he was not in a position to recognize the deep gulf between their piety and his own.

More to the point, it would never have occurred to him to look for such a gulf in the first place. He was expecting to find his own time and situation addressed more or less immediately in the Bible, and he was of course not alone in this. In the sixteenth century, scholars trained in the New Learning were suddenly alive to the importance of studying the ancient documents in their original languages and from the oldest available manuscripts, but they had not yet had time to develop a real sense of historical and cultural distance.

They were, to be sure, doing enough to alarm scholars of the Old Learning, who felt they had all they needed in the received tradition that gave them their license and warrant, and saw nothing to be gained—and much to be lost—by allowing a younger generation of scholars to test it. But the conflicts between them did not focus on the problem of historical distance; they approached the sources in much the same way, expecting biblical and classical writings to correlate quite directly with the life and thought of the sixteenth century.

Two matters above all stand out in this connection, and they involve the two aspects of the psalms that most particularly drew Calvin's interest and concern: their perception of themselves and their perception of God. In each case, lacking a more developed sense of historical distance, there was a very significant dissonance he was not able to hear.

Dissonance in Perceptions of Self

Calvin took it for granted that the psalmists were caught up in internal conflicts and the complex life of the psyche, and were therefore profoundly introspective. The decisive issue for prayer and faith is how well the intellective and immortal soul succeeds in subduing involuntary thoughts and feelings "according to the flesh." If one were to try to make a case for this—Calvin simply assumes it—one would surely appeal first to Psalm 42+43, where an address to the *nepeš* (for the sake of economy usually but inadequately translated "soul" or "self") appears three times as a refrain. As we listen to the address, which begins "Why are you cast down, O my soul?," we cannot miss the inner struggle in which the psalmist is engaged. In his commentary Calvin made as much of it as he could, but in fact it is far different from the kind of introspection he was assuming for the Psalter.

Even if the refrain is an aside, God is surely meant to overhear it.[11] By including it the psalmist effectively calls two things to God's attention. The first, an obvious appeal for pity, is that the psalmist has to deal with a *nepeš* that has an affective life of its own and is even more distressed by persistent misfortune than the psalmist is.[12] But God should also know that the psalmist has not given up, and is even now encouraging the despondent *nepeš* with the one means available, i.e., with the assurance that God will indeed grant the petition the psalmist is at this very moment putting to God ("Hope in God, for I shall again praise him . . ."). Each of these points is of course meant to move God to show favor; when God takes note of them both can help be far away?

The problem here does not lie in a faulty or blameworthy nepeš, and reforming or redeeming the *nepeš* is not the solution the psalmist is seeking. The problem is the psalmist's situation, vividly

11. I regard it as an integral part of the prayer, addressed to God indirectly. There is no reason I can see for supposing the address to the *nepeš* interrupts the prayer, or that the psalmist introduces it to gather courage before continuing to pray. The psalmists' manner throughout the Psalter does not at all suggest they were overwhelmed by the divine majesty or reluctant to press their appeals in prayer, and if we should choose to regard Psalm 42+43 as an exception to this general rule it would be hard to explain why the psalm repeats the refrain once again at the close, after the prayer has ended.

12. Note that the "I" who speaks represents itself as fully and firmly confident, unlike the *nepeš* it addresses. Psalm 131 takes a similar stance but presents it as a report instead of an inner conversation; the psalmist comes to God having already "calmed and quieted" his or her own *nepeš* as a mother does a weaned child.

portrayed in the prayer. Under the circumstances, the reaction of the *nepeš* is neither unreasonable nor unexpected; anyone's *nepeš* would feel much the same and need encouragement rather than censure. The second point is that the solution will not come until God responds to the prayer and changes the situation, and the *nepeš* (and the psalmist) are relieved of their troubles. Should this fail to happen, the psalmist will have nothing to show for having labored so hard to persevere, and the already disquieted *nepeš* may very well say "told you so."

Psalm 42+43 suffices to show that the psalmists could certainly speak of their inner state, and that they even had a conventional form for articulating it. Since the psalm is exceptional and the convention seldom employed, however, it appears they did not often find occasion to do so. In fact while no one would suggest for a moment that they are reticent to express their thoughts and feelings—they speak freely and often at length about their joys and sorrows, hopes and frustrations, loyalties and hatreds—they are not much given to introspection. As they choose to represent it in prayer, at least, their inner life is not in conflict, rarely torn by ambivalent or contrary thoughts and feelings. There is nothing in the Psalter, for example, comparable to the cry of the distraught father in Mark 9:24, "I believe; help my unbelief!"

In their prayers the psalmists do not engage in deeply-probing introspection in order to discover what they truly think or how they really feel; they speak as though they have no doubt about it, and declare it simply and directly. Neither do they engage in critical self-examination. They do not search their inner selves for hidden motivations or repressed feelings, just as they do not wonder whether their enemies may have some good in them after all. It is instructive in this regard that the psalmists do not petition for inward graces such as faith, trust, patience, hope, and perseverance, and rarely admit to a deficiency in such matters. Quite the opposite, when they speak of such graces they regularly talk as though they already possess them, and put them forward as one of their claims upon God's attention and favor.[13]

---

13. This is an essential point missed by E. K. Kim (1985) in his otherwise helpful study, as it has been by many others. As a result the role of trust in the

In all this it is impossible to know how much they are with-holding; this may be a stance they assume as a part of their strategy of persuasion, and not their actual experience. But even if this is so, Calvin's portrait of the psalmists is no longer recognizable. Either their self-perception is far less conflicted than he represented it, or they do not often feel it necessary or appropriate to pour out their innermost feelings in prayer. Why did he suppose otherwise? There are at least two factors that may help to account for it: on the one hand he accepted without question the Church's traditional anthropology, on the other he was anticipating a more complex understanding of the self, and he was reading both into the psalms.

The anthropology has been characterized by the Swiss theologian Karl Barth, himself a distinguished exponent of the tradition of Calvin, as an "abstractly dualistic conception" of soul and body that has its roots in the Greek philosophical tradition "but which unfortunately must also be described as the traditional Christian view" (1960a: 3, 380). Barth (1960a: 3, 384) noted that it had been challenged in Calvin's lifetime in a work published (in 1516) by an Italian philosopher, and regretted that Reformation theology did not at least take this occasion to gird itself for a new understanding; instead Calvin identified himself with the categorical Roman Catholic rejection of the thesis (*Inst.* 1.5.6). "Is it not clear," Barth asked, "that in these circumstances soul and body neither have nor can have anything in common, but can only be in conflict and finally part from one another?" (1960a: 3, 380). But if this was formative for Calvin, it was not an issue for the psalmists; they would not even have understood the presumption of duality that gives rise to it.

The second factor is at least equally important. Calvin, like Luther, was personally acquainted with intense and deeply-probing introspection, and it has been said of them both that they sensed so fully the complexity of psychic life that they anticipated the discovery of the unconscious and many of the specific mechanisms of Freudian psychology (Selinger 1984: 46–47). Calvin's distinctive personal response to this, in many respects quite different from Luther's, seems to have made him unusually well-fitted to address

piety of the prayer psalms is misconstrued; the psalmists do not struggle to achieve it, they set out to capitalize on it.

the deepest concerns and longings of the middle third of the sixteenth century, and it is doubtless one of the reasons his writings
continue to speak to many in the present. By applying his insight
so brilliantly to the psalms, he provided the Church with a mode
of appropriation that has been of lasting significance. It was, however, an anachronism to read it into the psalms and to take it for
granted that self-knowledge, and more precisely the knowledge of
sin, was as central a problem for the psalmists as it was for Luther
and himself.

For the most part the resistance the psalmists were seeking
so earnestly to overcome by prayer they did not perceive in themselves, but in God. They aimed to improve their situation, not by
reforming their attitude toward God, but by cultivating a more favorable disposition on God's part toward themselves.

Dissonance in Perceptions of God

It is not only the psalmists' approaches and responses to God that
are different from Calvin's, however. The root of the matter lies
deeper. There are marked differences in their perceptions of God
as well, and therefore in the attitudes they take toward God and
toward what God does to them and for them. As others have noted,
this is a critical issue that even modern biblical scholars have been
slow to recognize.[14]

In my view if we are to understand what the Hebrew Bible
thinks about God, we must first understand *how* it thinks about
God. And this is not a great mystery: it thinks with precisely those
anthropomorphic and sociomorphic images Calvin was at such

14. Cf. Terence Fretheim (1984: 17): "As one surveys the landscape of OT
scholarship on the understanding of God, the portrait of God which normally
emerges bears a striking resemblance to the quite traditional Jewish or Christian understanding of God regnant in synagogue or church. Save for matters
relating to historical development . . . , one can read back and forth between
church dogmatics textbooks and most God-talk in OT studies without missing
a beat." I think this is apt, although I am inclined to think that Judaism has
preserved more of the biblical perception than the Church has. However that
may be, Fretheim's book is a very good start. He goes beyond biblical thought,
however, when he represents this as God's self-imposed limitation.

pains to rationalize. It does not think in the abstract categorical terms that have long been traditional in Western theology. As a result, the very perception of God among ancient Israelites was fundamentally different from Calvin's. That is why they did not shy as he did from imagining God in many respects like themselves, or from acting upon this in approaching God in prayer. Not least among these likenesses were the affective aspects of experience, and they took it for granted these were as important to God as they were to themselves.

If Calvin found grounds for confidence in the vast gulf that separates heaven and earth—it serves, for one thing, to insulate the divine realm from all human contingencies and infirmities—it was the likeness and sympathy between them that more often encouraged and comforted the psalmists. When it occurred to them, as it sometimes did, that at some points there may be no common ground, they found the thought alarming and did what they could to bring the matter to God's attention. A God in whose sight "a thousand years . . . are like yesterday when it is past" (Ps 90:4, cf. vv. 1–2), for example, may not entirely understand what it is like to have the very limited life expectancy of a mortal (Ps 90:3, 5–6, 11–12); as a result, God may not fully realize how devastating the punishing divine wrath actually is (Ps 90:7–10). The petition that follows is appropriate to this appeal: God is asked to restore some semblance of balance by showing compassion and favor to them now (Ps 90:13–17; note esp. v. 15). A prayer of this sort was incomprehensible to Calvin, except as an example of human frailty; in its own context it was fully in keeping with accepted piety.

In his later years Karl Barth, reflecting self-critically upon his own earlier preoccupation with God as the "Wholly Other," expressed the wish that Calvin had given more attention to the humanity of God. "His Geneva would then not have become such a gloomy affair. His letters would then not have contained so much bitterness" (Barth 1960b: 49). My attention was drawn to the passage by W. Fred Graham, who cites it in his book *The Constructive Revolutionary* (1971: 182). Barth (1960b: 49) appealed to the Incarnation as the corrective. "It is when we look at Jesus Christ that we know decisively that God's deity does not exclude, but includes His *humanity.*" "My own reflection," Graham writes, "is that Calvin was true to Chalcedon, that he followed scholastic theology, and that the difficulty lies with the impossible task which Chalcedon presents to the biblical theologian" (1971: 183). In a footnote he adds, "Perhaps if this were a study of theology proper we would need to ask if the idea of God held by the bishops of the fifth century admits of a solution which can be correlated with the New Testament witness to the God of Israel and the Father of Jesus Christ. Can God—the unchangeable, immutable, impassible—relate seriously to time-fettered humanity or bring any new thing to pass? Is the God of Chalcedon and Calvin recognizable in the Bible?" (Graham 1971: 239 n.16)

By implication Graham reaches behind the Christological declarations of Chalcedon in the fifth century to the underlying perception of God the councils were presupposing. That is where the issue lies for those who wish to understand the Psalms, and indeed the Hebrew Bible.

6

In Conclusion

IN THE END THE issue is not whether Calvin was justified in taking
the approach to the prayer psalms he did, but whether it is any longer defensible. As I study his exposition of their piety I find much
that I recognize in the work of my colleagues in biblical studies at
the present time. He has helped me to understand the approach
they have taken, and why it is so different from my own. He has
not, however, persuaded me that it is a convincing reading of these
psalms on their own terms, or helped me to understand why my
colleagues go as far as they do to perpetuate it.[1] No doubt there are
some things in every age that cannot be seen because they must
not be seen—the cost would be too great to bear. But the loss also
exacts its own price, and perhaps this is one of the tragedies of
human existence. If so, it is one we can hardly expect to escape

---

1. Part of the motivation has been the complaint that "modern critical
study is so pledged to an ideal of objectivity and neutrality with respect to the
text, and so occupied with a notion of past history as the strange and alien"
that it is "boring" (Mays 1990: 203). If it is, the problem lies not in the method
itself but in the tendency of modern critical scholars to ignore (or shy from?)
the study of biblical piety, which is anything but boring. Reading the psalms in
one's own mirror, as Calvin did, is defensible as long as one does it admittedly
and intentionally (this is what Mays has in mind), but closing the "hermeneutical circle" in this way also exacts the price Calvin paid: it is far more difficult
for the psalms to speak for themselves.

ourselves. But that gives us no license to continue to ignore what others could not see.

Calvin was an extraordinarily able and convincing interpreter of the Psalter in his own setting; in that sense his reading of the book was undeniably true. Furthermore, he was not deaf to the dissonance between the prayer psalms and his own convictions about due and proper prayer; that is what makes him such an interesting figure to study. At the same time the ethos and imperatives of his time and situation made it virtually impossible for him to recognize that the prayer psalms represented a piety in so many respects alien to his own.

Since he could hear, but not listen to, the quite different voice of the psalmists he proceeded to harmonize it with his own, and he accomplished this by transposing the prayer psalms into another, more familiar and congenial mode. As a result, whatever he might have learned from these psalms they were unable to teach him. They could not make themselves understood in their own voice, but merely echo his own. When this happens there is always a price to be paid. There is much to be learned from the biblical tradition if it is allowed to speak for itself, and is not simply used as a vehicle to proclaim what its readers have already decided it must say.

The legacy Calvin left to future generations was unquestionably rich, but this is one of its weaknesses. Because it was an historical orientation with only the most limited sense of social and cultural distance, typical of the sixteenth century, it tended to confirm and perpetuate the belief that the piety of Psalter, indeed of the Bible—its perceptions, concerns, attitudes and responses—was in every essential way a mirror of Western Christian, and especially Calvin's newly formulated Reformed piety. This is patently an ahistorical view even if it presents itself in historical guise.

This is by no means to suggest that all the problems faced by Church and Synagogue would be solved if they were simply to be more biblical. The humanity of God is an important theological issue; the psalms and other biblical books raise it, they can help us think about it, but they cannot resolve it for us by themselves. Calvin himself models the risks we run when we try to abstract elements from someone else's piety and appropriate them for ourselves.

There are Christian poets in the Third World, Ernesto Cardinal[2] among them, who seem to be able to respond more immediately and fully to many aspects of the piety of the Psalter than we have been able to manage in American and European churches. There is no doubt something we can learn from them. But if we do no more than to recognize that our own piety is not simply interchangeable with biblical piety, and that there are other pieties appropriately and responsibly different from our own, it may at least be a beginning. It ought to make us more patient with each other, and a little less arrogant about ourselves.

2. The poems in Ernesto Cardinal's *Salmos* (1969) are modeled on biblical psalms. Cardinal was a novice under Thomas Merton in the Monastery of Our Lady of Gethsemane, who was subsequently ordained a priest in Nicaragua and served as Minister of Culture there.

Bibliography

Balentine, Samuel E. 1993. *Prayer in the Hebrew Bible: The Drama of Divine-Human Dialogue*. Overtures to Biblical Theology. Minneapolis: Fortress.

Barth, Karl. 1936–1977. *Church Dogmatics*. Translated by G. T. Thompson et al. Edinburgh: T. & T. Clark.

———. 1960. *The Humanity of God*. Richmond: John Knox.

———. 2002. *Prayer: 50th Anniversary Edition*. Edited by Don E. Sailers. Louisville: Westminster John Knox.

Broyles, Craig C. 1988. *The Conflict of Faith and Experience in the Psalms: A Form-Critical and Theological Study*. Journal for the Study of the Old Testament Supplement Series 52. Sheffield: JSOT Press.

Brueggemann, Walter. 1984. *The Message of the Psalms: A Theological Commentary*. Augsburg Old Testament Studies. Minneapolis: Augsburg.

———. 1985. "A Shape for Old Testament Theology I: Structure Legitmation." *Catholic Biblical Quarterly* 47:28–46.

———. 1985. "A Shape for Old Testament Theology II: Embrace of Pain." *Catholic Biblical Quarterly* 47:395–415.

———. 2009. *An Unsettling God: The Heart of the Hebrew Bible*. Minneapolis: Fortress.

Calvin, John. 1845–1849. *Commentary on the Book of Psalms*. 5 vols. Edited by J. Anderson. Edinburgh: The Calvin Translation Society.

———. 1926–1970. *Joannis Calvini, Opera Selecta*. 5 vols. Edited by P. Barth and W. Niesel. Munich: Kaiser.

———. 1960. *Institutes of the Christian Religion* [1559 edition]. 2 vols. Edited by J. T. McNeill. Translated by Ford Lewis Battles. Philadelphia: Westminster.

———. 1965. *A Commentary on the Psalms*. Vol. 1. Translated by A. Golding, 1571. Revised and edited by T. H. L. Parker in 1962. London: James Clarke.

———. 1975. *Institutes of the Christian Religion* [1536 edition]. Translated by Ford Lewis Battles. Atlanta: John Knox.

Cardinal, Ernesto. 1969. *Salmos*. Buenos Aires: Carlos Lohle.

Childs, Brevard S. 1989. "The Struggle for God's Righteousness in the Psalter." In *Christ in Our Place: The Humanity of God in Christ for the Reconciliation of the World*, edited by Trevor A. Hart and Daniel P. Thimell, 255–64. Princeton Theological Monograph Series 25. Exter, UK: Paternoster.

Dowey, Edward A. Jr. 1952. *The Knowledge of God in Calvin's Theology*. New York: Columbia University Press.

Driver, Daniel R. 2010. *Brevard Childs, Biblical Theologian: For the Church's One Bible*. Forschungen zum Alten Testament 2/46. Tübingen: Mohr/Siebeck.

Fretheim, Terence E. 1984. *The Suffering of God: An Old Testament Perspective*. Overtures to Biblical Theology. Philadelphia: Fortress.

Gerstenberger, Erhard S. 2010. *Der bittende Mensch: Bittritual und Klagelied des Ein-zelnen im Alten Testament*. 1980. Reprinted, Eugene, OR: Wipf & Stock.

Graham, Fred. 1971. *The Constructive Revolutionary: John Calvin & His Socio-economic Impact*. Richmond: John Knox.

Greenberg, Moshe. 1983. *Biblical Prose Prayer: As a Window to the Popular Religion of Ancient Israel*. The Taubman Lectures in Jewish Studies, Sixth Series. Berkeley: University of Californmia Press.

Heschel, Abraham. 1962. *The Prophets*. New York: Harper & Row.

Hesselink, John. 2002. "Karl Barth on Prayer." In *Prayer: 50th Anniversary Edition*, edited by Don E. Sailers, 74–94. Louisville: Westminster John Knox.

Hobbs, R. Gerald. 1984. "How Firm a Foundation: Martin Bucer's Historical Exegesis of the Psalms." *Church History* 53: 477–91.

———. 1990. "*Hebraica Veritas* and *Traditio Apostolica*: Saint Paul and the Interpretation of the Psalms in the Sixteenth Century." In *The Bible in the Sixteenth Century*, edited by David C. Steinmetz, 83–99. Durham: Duke University Press.

Jones, Serene. 1993. "This God Which Is Not One: Irigaray and Barth on the Divine." In *Transfigurations: Theology and the French Feminists*, edited by C. W. Maggie Kim et al., 109–41. Minneapolis: Fortress.

Jung, Kyu Nam. 1979. "Court Etiquette in the Old Testament." PhD diss., Drew University.

Kaltner, John, and Louis Stulman, editors. 2004. *Inspired Speech: Prophecy in the Ancient Near East; Essays in Honour of Herbert B. Huffmon*. London: T. & T. Clark.

Kim, Ee Kon. 1985. *The Rapid Change of Mood in the Lament Psalms: A Matrix for the Establishment of a Psalm Theology*. Seoul: Korea Theological Study Institute.

Kitamori, Kazoh. 2005. *The Theology of the Pain of God*. 1965. Reprinted, Eugene, OR: Wipf & Stock.

Kraus, Hans-Joachim. 1986. *Theology of the Psalms*. Translated by Keith Crim. Continental Commentaries. Minneapolis: Augsburg.

———. 1988. *Psalms 1–59: A Commentary*. Translated by Hilton C. Oswald. Continental Commentaries. Minneapolis: Augsburg.

———. 1989. *Psalms 60–150: A Commentary*. Translated by Hilton C. Oswald. Continental Commentaries. Minneapolis: Augsburg.

Lindstrom, Fredrik. 1994. *Suffering and Sin: Interpretations of Illness in the Individual Complaint Psalms*. Coniectanea Biblica Old Testament Series 37. Stockholm: Almqvist & Wiksell.

Mays, James Luther. 1990. "Calvin's Commentary on the Psalms: The Preface as Introduction." In *John Calvin and the Church: A Prism of Reform*, edited by Timothy George, 195–204. Louisville: Westminster John Knox.

Miller, Patrick D. 1986. *Interpreting the Psalms*. Philadelphia: Fortress.

———. 1993. "Prayer as Persuasion: The Rhetoric and Intention of Prayer." *Word & World* 13: 356–62.

———. 1994. *They Cried to the Lord: The Form and Theology of Biblical Prayer*. Minneapolis: Fortress.

Moltmann, Jürgen. 1974. *The Crucified God: The Cross as the Foundation and Criticism of Christian Theology*. Translated by R. A. Wilson and John Bowden. New York: Harper & Row.

Pak, G. Sujin. 2010. *The Judaizing Calvin: Sixteenth-Century Debates over the Messianic Psalms*. Oxford: Oxford University Press.

Parker, T. H. L. 1986. *Calvin's Old Testament Commentaries*. Edinburgh: T. & T. Clark.

Petuchowski, Jacob J. 1972. *Understanding Jewish Prayer*. New York: Ktav.

Ringgren, Helmer. 1963. *The Faith of the Psalmists*. Philadelphia: Fortress.

Roberts, J. J. M. 1975. "Divine Freedom and Cultic Manipulation in Israel and Mesopotamia." In *Unity and Diversity: Essays in the History, Literature, and Religion of the Ancient Near East*, edited by H. Goedicke and J. J. M. Roberts, 181–90. The Johns Hopkins Near Eastern Studies. Baltimore: Johns Hopkins University Press.

Selinger, Suzanne. 1984. *Calvin against Himself: An Inquiry in Intellectual History*. Hamden, CT: Archon.

Weiser, Artur. 1962. *The Psalms: A Commentary*. Translated by Herbert Hartwell. Old Testament Library. Philadelphia: Westminster.

Wendel, François. 1963. *Calvin: The Origins and Development of His Religious Thought*. New York: Harper & Row.

Westermaann, Claus. 1981. *Praise and Lament in the Psalms*. Translated by Keith R. Crim and Richard N. Soulen. Atlanta: John Knox.

———. 1989. *The Living Psalms*. Translated by J. R. Porter. Grand Rapids: Eerdmans.

Index of Calvin's Works

Index of Calvin's Works

Index of Names

Index of Names

Scripture Index

~

NEW TESTAMENT

Mark

Luke

1 John

~

BABYLONIAN TALMUD

Sanhedrin